Table of Contents

Chapter 1: Crafting the Perfect Resume ... 17
1.1 Understanding the Purpose of a Resume ... 17
1.2 Resume Formats: Which One is Right for You? ... 17
1.2.1 Reverse-Chronological Resume ... 17
1.2.2 Functional Resume ... 18
1.2.3 Combination Resume ... 18
1.3 The Anatomy of a Great Resume ... 18
1.3.1 Contact Information ... 18
1.3.2 Summary or Objective Statement ... 19
1.3.3 Work Experience ... 19
1.3.4 Education ... 20
1.3.5 Skills ... 20
1.4 Tailoring Your Resume to Each Job ... 20
1.4.1 Analyze the Job Description ... 20
1.4.2 Match Your Resume to the Job ... 21
1.5 The Importance of Formatting and Design ... 21
1.6 Common Resume Mistakes to Avoid ... 21

Chapter 2: Crafting a Cover Letter That Stands Out ... 22
2.1 The Purpose of a Cover Letter ... 22
2.2 Structuring Your Cover Letter ... 22
2.2.1 Contact Information and Header ... 22
2.2.2 Salutation ... 23
2.2.3 Introduction: Grab Their Attention ... 23
2.2.4 Body: Connect Your Skills to the Job ... 23
2.3 Customizing Your Cover Letter ... 24
2.3.1 Research the Company ... 24
2.3.2 Reflect the Job Description ... 25
2.4 Conclusion: Closing with a Call to Action ... 25
2.5 Common Mistakes to Avoid ... 25
2.5.1 Generic Language ... 26
2.5.2 Restating Your Resume ... 26
2.5.3 Focusing on What You Want ... 26
2.5.4 Being Too Long or Too Short ... 26
2.6 Proofreading and Finalizing Your Cover Letter ... 26
2.6.1 Proofread Multiple Times ... 26

- 2.6.2 Get a Second Opinion 26
- 2.6.3 Ensure Consistency with Your Resume 27
- 2.7 How to Handle Different Types of Cover Letters 27
  - 2.7.1 Applying for a Job Online 27
  - 2.7.2 Cold Outreach or Unadvertised Jobs 27
  - 2.7.3 Internal Job Applications 28
  - 2.7.4 Applying to Startups or Creative Industries 28
  - 2.7.5 When There's No Requirement for a Cover Letter 29
- 2.8 Tailoring for Specific Industries 29
  - 2.8.1 Technology and Engineering 29
  - 2.8.2 Healthcare 29
  - 2.8.3 Sales and Marketing 30
- 2.9 Leveraging Technology in Your Cover Letter 30
  - 2.9.1 Including Hyperlinks 30
  - 2.9.2 Incorporating Digital Media 30

Chapter 3: Job Search Strategies: Navigating the Modern Job Market 32

- 3.1 The Importance of a Targeted Job Search 32
  - 3.1.1 Identify Your Career Goals 32
  - 3.1.2 Research Potential Employers 32
- 3.2 Leveraging Job Boards and Online Platforms 32
  - 3.2.1 General Job Boards 33
  - 3.2.2 Niche Job Boards 33
  - 3.2.3 Company Websites 33
  - 3.2.4 Aggregators 34
- 3.3 Maximizing LinkedIn for Job Search Success 34
  - 3.3.1 Optimizing Your LinkedIn Profile 34
  - 3.3.2 Using LinkedIn Jobs 34
  - 3.3.3 Engaging with Recruiters and Networking on LinkedIn 35
- 3.4 Networking: The Key to Hidden Job Opportunities 35
  - 3.4.1 Expanding Your Network 35
  - 3.4.2 Reaching Out to Your Existing Network 35
  - 3.4.3 Informational Interviews 36
- 3.5 Job Fairs and Networking Events 36
  - 3.5.2 Maximizing Your Time at a Job Fair 36
  - 3.5.3 Following Up After a Job Fair 37
- 3.6 Cold Outreach and Direct Applications 37

- 3.6.1 What is Cold Outreach? 37
- 3.6.2 How to Write a Cold Outreach Email 37
- 3.7 Standing Out in a Competitive Job Market 38
  - 3.7.1 Building a Personal Brand 38
  - 3.7.2 Volunteering or Freelancing 39
  - 3.7.3 Get Certified or Take Courses 39
- 3.8 Tracking Your Job Applications 39
  - 3.8.1 Create a Job Application Tracker 39
  - 3.8.2 Follow-Up on Applications 40

Chapter 4: Interviewing with Confidence: Mastering the Art of the Job Interview 41

- 4.1 Preparing for the Interview 41
  - 4.1.1 Research the Company 41
  - 4.1.2 Review the Job Description 41
  - 4.1.3 Prepare Your Responses to Common Interview Questions 42
- 4.2 The STAR Method: Answering Behavioral Questions 42
- 4.3 Preparing Questions for the Interviewer 43
- 4.4 The Day of the Interview: Making a Great First Impression 43
  - 4.4.1 Dress Appropriately 44
  - 4.4.2 Arrive on Time 44
  - 4.4.3 Bring the Necessary Materials 44
  - 4.4.4 Nonverbal Communication 44
- 4.5 Handling Different Types of Interviews 45
  - 4.5.1 Phone Interviews 45
  - 4.5.2 Video Interviews 45
  - 4.5.3 Panel Interviews 45
  - 4.5.4 Group Interviews 46
  - 4.5.5 Case or Problem-Solving Interviews 46
- 4.6 How to Handle Tough Interview Questions 46
  - 4.6.1 "What is your greatest weakness?" 46
  - 4.6.2 "Why did you leave your last job?" 47
  - 4.6.3 "Tell me about a time you failed." 47
- 4.7 What to Do After the Interview: Following Up 48
  - 4.7.1 Send a Thank-You Email 48
  - 4.7.2 Following Up on the Status of Your Application 48

Chapter 5: The Follow-Up: Navigating Post-Interview Communication and Offers 50

- 5.1 The Importance of Following Up After an Interview 50

- 5.1.1 Reiterating Your Interest 50
- 5.1.2 Showcasing Your Professionalism 50
- 5.1.3 Offering Additional Information 50
- 5.2 How and When to Send a Thank-You Email 50
  - 5.2.1 When to Send Your Thank-You Email 51
  - 5.2.2 What to Include in Your Thank-You Email 51
  - 5.2.3 Handwritten Notes vs. Email 52
- 5.3 Following Up on the Status of Your Application 52
  - 5.3.1 When to Follow Up 52
  - 5.3.2 How to Follow Up 52
  - 5.3.3 What to Do If You Don't Hear Back 52
- 5.4 Handling Job Offers 53
  - 5.4.1 Reviewing the Job Offer 53
  - 5.4.2 Handling Multiple Job Offers 53
- 5.5 Negotiating Salary and Benefits 54
  - 5.5.1 Preparing for Salary Negotiation 54
  - 5.5.2 How to Negotiate Salary 54
  - 5.5.3 Negotiating Benefits 54
- 5.6 Accepting or Declining a Job Offer 55
  - 5.6.1 How to Accept a Job Offer 55
  - 5.6.2 How to Decline a Job Offer 55
- 5.7 Making the Right Career Decision 56
  - 5.7.1 Culture and Work-Life Balance 56
  - 5.7.2 Long-Term Growth Potential 56
  - 5.7.3 Job Stability and Security 56
  - 5.7.4 Location and Commute 57
  - 5.7.5 Compensation and Benefits Package 57

Chapter 6: Negotiating a Job Offer: Maximizing Your Compensation and Benefits 58
- 6.1 Why You Should Negotiate 58
  - 6.1.1 The Benefits of Negotiating 58
  - 6.1.2 Overcoming the Fear of Negotiation 58
- 6.2 Preparing for Salary Negotiation 59
  - 6.2.1 Research the Market 59
  - 6.2.2 Assess Your Value 59
  - 6.2.3 Decide on Your Salary Range 60
- 6.3 The Negotiation Conversation 60

6.3.1 When to Bring Up Salary Negotiation 60

6.3.2 How to Negotiate Salary 60

6.3.3 How to Negotiate Benefits 61

6.3.4 Responding to Common Employer Reactions 61

6.4 Negotiating in Special Circumstances 61

6.4.1 Negotiating as a Recent Graduate or Early-Career Professional 62

6.4.2 Negotiating During an Economic Downturn 62

6.4.3 Negotiating a Promotion or Raise 62

6.5 Finalizing the Negotiation 63

6.5.1 Confirming the Offer in Writing 63

6.5.2 Expressing Gratitude 63

6.6 Knowing When to Walk Away 63

6.6.1 Signs It's Time to Walk Away 64

6.6.2 How to Decline an Offer Respectfully 64

Chapter 7: Starting a New Job Successfully: Making a Positive First Impression and Building Long-Term Success 66

7.1 Preparing for Your First Day 66

7.1.1 Confirm the Details 66

7.1.2 Organize Your Paperwork 66

7.1.3 Get a Good Night's Sleep 66

7.2 Making a Positive First Impression 67

7.2.1 Be Punctual 67

7.2.2 Be Polite and Professional 67

7.2.3 Show Enthusiasm 67

7.2.4 Listen and Observe 67

7.3 Navigating the Onboarding Process 68

7.3.1 Understand the Onboarding Timeline 68

7.3.2 Ask for Clarification 68

7.3.3 Learn the Company's Systems and Tools 68

7.3.4 Meet with Key Stakeholders 68

7.4 Building Strong Relationships with Your Team 69

7.4.1 Be Open and Approachable 69

7.4.2 Offer Help 69

7.4.3 Respect Team Dynamics 69

7.4.4 Communicate Effectively 69

7.5 Setting Goals for Your First 90 Days 70

- 7.5.1 Understand Your Manager's Expectations 70
- 7.5.2 Set Short-Term and Long-Term Goals 70
- 7.5.3 Create a 30-60-90 Day Plan 71
- 7.6 Seeking Feedback and Continuous Improvement 71
  - 7.6.1 Ask for Feedback Regularly 71
  - 7.6.2 Be Open to Constructive Criticism 71
  - 7.6.3 Track Your Progress 72
- 7.7 Managing Work-Life Balance in a New Role 72
  - 7.7.1 Set Boundaries Early 72
  - 7.7.2 Avoid Overcommitting 72
  - 7.7.3 Make Time for Breaks 73
- 7.8 Dealing with Challenges in a New Role 73
  - 7.8.1 Navigating Unclear Expectations 73
  - 7.8.2 Handling Miscommunications 73
  - 7.8.3 Overcoming Imposter Syndrome 73

Chapter 8: Setting Yourself Up for Long-Term Career Growth: Advancing in Your Role and Developing Key Skills 75

- 8.1 Defining Your Career Goals 75
  - 8.1.1 Setting SMART Career Goals 75
  - 8.1.2 Identifying Short-Term and Long-Term Goals 76
- 8.2 Developing Key Skills for Career Growth 76
  - 8.2.1 Hard Skills vs. Soft Skills 76
  - 8.2.2 Identifying Skills You Need to Develop 77
  - 8.2.3 Pursuing Professional Development 77
- 8.3 Seeking Opportunities for Advancement 78
  - 8.3.1 Take Initiative and Be Proactive 78
  - 8.3.2 Network Within Your Organization 78
  - 8.3.3 Find a Mentor or Sponsor 79
- 8.4 Building a Strong Professional Network 79
  - 8.4.1 Networking Strategies 79
  - 8.4.2 Leveraging LinkedIn for Career Growth 79
- 8.5 Embracing Continuous Learning and Adaptability 80
  - 8.5.1 Stay Informed About Industry Trends 80
  - 8.5.2 Adapt to New Technologies 81
  - 8.5.3 Commit to Lifelong Learning 81
- 8.6 Building Your Personal Brand 81

- 8.6.1 Define Your Brand 81
- 8.6.2 Build an Online Presence 82
- 8.6.3 Be Consistent 82

Chapter 9: Leadership and Team Dynamics: Leading Effectively and Contributing to a Positive Workplace Culture 83

- 9.1.1 The Difference Between Leadership and Management 83
- 9.1.2 Leadership Styles 83
- 9.2 Essential Leadership Skills 84
  - 9.2.1 Emotional Intelligence (EQ) 84
  - 9.2.2 Effective Communication 84
  - 9.2.3 Decision-Making 85
  - 9.2.4 Delegation 85
  - 9.2.5 Conflict Resolution 86
- 9.3 Building Strong Team Dynamics 86
  - 9.3.1 Building Trust 86
  - 9.3.2 Encouraging Collaboration 86
  - 9.3.3 Recognizing and Celebrating Success 87
- 9.4 Fostering a Positive Workplace Culture 87
  - 9.4.1 Lead by Example 87
  - 9.4.2 Promote Inclusivity and Diversity 88
  - 9.4.3 Encourage Open Communication 88
  - 9.4.4 Support Employee Development 88
- 9.5 Leading Through Change 89
  - 9.5.1 Communicate the Vision 89
  - 9.5.2 Provide Support During Transitions 89
  - 9.5.3 Stay Positive and Resilient 90

Chapter 10: Maintaining a Healthy Work-Life Balance: Balancing Career Ambitions with Personal Well-Being 91

- 10.1.1 The Importance of Work-Life Balance 91
- 10.1.2 Signs of an Imbalance 91
- 10.2 Setting Boundaries 92
  - 10.2.1 Setting Work Hours 92
  - 10.2.2 Establishing Personal Boundaries 92
  - 10.2.3 Managing Remote Work Boundaries 93
- 10.3 Time Management Strategies 93
  - 10.3.1 Prioritizing Tasks 93

- 10.3.2 Time Blocking 93
- 10.3.3 Avoiding Multitasking 94
- 10.4 Avoiding Burnout 94
  - 10.4.1 Recognizing the Signs of Burnout 94
  - 10.4.2 Strategies for Preventing Burnout 95
  - 10.4.3 Seeking Support 95
- 10.5 Integrating Self-Care into Your Routine 95
  - 10.5.1 Physical Self-Care 96
  - 10.5.2 Mental and Emotional Self-Care 96
  - 10.5.3 Social Self-Care 96
- 10.6 Balancing Personal Goals with Career Ambitions 97
  - 10.6.1 Aligning Career Goals with Personal Values 97
  - 10.6.2 Making Time for Personal Growth 97

Chapter 11: Navigating Career Transitions: Successfully Changing Careers, Industries, or Roles 99
- 11.1 Identifying When It's Time for a Career Change 99
  - 11.1.1 Signs It's Time for a Career Change 99
  - 11.1.2 Evaluating Your Readiness for Change 100
- 11.2 Planning for a Career Transition 100
  - 11.2.1 Setting Clear Goals 100
  - 11.2.2 Building the Necessary Skills 101
  - 11.2.3 Networking in Your Desired Industry 101
- 11.3 Making a Smooth Transition 102
  - 11.3.1 Updating Your Resume and LinkedIn Profile 102
  - 11.3.2 Adjusting to a New Role or Industry 102
  - 11.3.3 Managing Uncertainty During a Career Change 103
- 11.4 Overcoming Common Career Transition Challenges 103
  - 11.4.1 Dealing with Rejection 104
  - 11.4.2 Managing Imposter Syndrome 104
  - 11.4.3 Balancing Financial Stability During a Transition 104
- 11.5 Measuring Success in Your Career Transition 105
  - 11.5.1 Setting Transition Milestones 105
  - 11.5.2 Reflecting on Your Progress 105
  - 11.5.3 Celebrating Small Wins 106

Chapter 12: Developing a Personal and Professional Brand: Building and Maintaining a Strong Reputation 107
- 12.1 Understanding Personal Branding 107

- 12.1.1 Why Personal Branding Matters ... 107
- 12.1.2 The Key Elements of Personal Branding ... 107
- 12.2 Defining Your Personal Brand ... 108
  - 12.2.1 Self-Assessment ... 108
  - 12.2.2 Crafting Your Brand Statement ... 108
- 12.3 Building an Online Presence ... 109
  - 12.3.1 Optimizing Your LinkedIn Profile ... 109
  - 12.3.2 Creating a Personal Website ... 110
  - 12.3.3 Managing Your Online Reputation ... 110
- 12.4 Maintaining and Evolving Your Brand ... 110
  - 12.4.1 Regularly Updating Your Brand ... 111
  - 12.4.2 Adapting to Industry Trends ... 111
  - 12.4.3 Building a Strong Network to Support Your Brand ... 111
- 12.5 Leveraging Your Brand for Career Advancement ... 112
  - 12.5.1 Positioning Yourself for Promotions ... 112
  - 12.5.2 Attracting New Job Opportunities ... 113
  - 12.5.3 Leveraging Your Brand for Freelance or Entrepreneurial Ventures ... 113

Chapter 13: Navigating Workplace Politics: Building Positive Relationships and Advancing with Integrity ... 115

- 13.1 Understanding Workplace Politics ... 115
  - 13.1.1 The Role of Power and Influence ... 115
  - 13.1.2 Identifying Key Stakeholders ... 116
- 13.2 Building Strategic Relationships ... 116
  - 13.2.1 Cultivating Allies ... 116
  - 13.2.3 Networking Across Departments ... 117
- 13.3 Managing Conflicts and Power Struggles ... 118
  - 13.3.1 Handling Conflicts Professionally ... 118
  - 13.3.2 Avoiding Negative Office Politics ... 118
  - 13.3.3 Managing Power Struggles ... 119
- 13.4 Advancing Your Career with Integrity ... 119
  - 13.4.1 Leading with Integrity ... 119
  - 13.4.2 Navigating Promotions and Career Advancements Ethically ... 120
  - 13.4.3 Balancing Ambition with Team Success ... 120
- 13.5 Managing Office Politics in Remote or Hybrid Work Environments ... 121
  - 13.5.1 Building Relationships in a Remote Setting ... 121
  - 13.5.2 Managing Conflicts in a Remote Environment ... 121

13.5.3 Navigating Virtual Team Dynamics 121

Chapter 14: Managing Leadership Transitions: Succeeding as a New Leader 123

14.1 Preparing for a Leadership Role 123

14.1.1 Understanding Your New Responsibilities 123

14.1.2 Developing a Leadership Mindset 123

14.2 Building Trust with Your Team 124

14.2.1 Building Relationships with Team Members 124

14.2.2 Leading by Example 124

14.2.3 Encouraging Open Communication 125

14.3 Establishing Your Leadership Style 125

14.3.1 Identifying Your Leadership Style 125

14.3.2 Balancing Authority and Empowerment 126

14.3.3 Navigating Challenges as a New Leader 126

Chapter 15: Transitioning from Military to Civilian Life: A Guide for Service Members 128

15.1 Understanding the Challenges of Transitioning to Civilian Life 128

15.1.1 Common Challenges for Service Members 128

15.1.2 Preparing Mentally for the Transition 128

15.2 Leveraging Your Military Experience in Civilian Life 129

15.2.1 Translating Military Skills for Civilian Employers 129

15.2.2 Highlighting Your Soft Skills 129

15.3 Navigating the Civilian Job Market 130

15.3.1 Crafting a Civilian-Friendly Resume 130

15.3.2 Searching for Civilian Jobs 130

15.3.3 Interview Preparation for Veterans 131

15.4 Utilizing Transition Resources 131

15.4.1 TAP (Transition Assistance Program) 131

15.4.2 Veteran Service Organizations (VSOs) 132

15.4.3 Education and Training Benefits 132

15.5 Setting Goals for a Successful Transition 132

15.5.1 Career Goals 133

15.5.2 Personal and Financial Goals 133

15.5.3 Health and Well-Being Goals 133

15.6 Long-Term Success: Thriving in Civilian Life 134

15.6.1 Finding Purpose and Fulfillment 134

15.6.2 Staying Connected to the Veteran Community 134

Chapter 16: Navigating Career and Life as a Military Spouse Overseas 136

- 16.1 Understanding the Unique Challenges of Life Overseas 136
  - 16.1.1 Common Challenges for Military Spouses Overseas 136
  - 16.1.2 Embracing the Opportunities 136
- 16.2 Building a Portable Career 137
  - 16.2.1 Identifying Careers That Travel Well 137
  - 16.2.2 Leveraging Military Spouse Employment Programs 137
- 16.3 Navigating Local Job Markets and Employment Laws 138
  - 16.3.1 Understanding SOFA and Work Authorization 138
  - 16.3.2 Overcoming Language Barriers 139
- 16.4 Adapting to a New Culture and Maintaining Well-Being 139
  - 16.4.1 Embracing Cultural Differences 139
  - 16.4.2 Staying Connected with Loved Ones 139
  - 16.4.3 Prioritizing Self-Care and Mental Health 140
- 16.5 Leveraging Available Resources for Military Spouses 140
  - 16.5.1 Military OneSource 141
  - 16.5.2 Spouse Education and Career Opportunities (SECO) 141
  - 16.5.3 Installation-Specific Resources 141
- 16.6 Setting Goals for Your Overseas 142
  - 16.6.1 Personal Growth and Learning 142
  - 16.6.2 Career Development 142
  - 16.6.3 Family and Community Involvement 143

Chapter 17: Navigating the Federal Employment Process: A Guide for Military Service Members, Veterans, Military Spouses, and Civilians 144

- 17.1 Understanding the Federal Hiring Process 144
  - 17.1.1 Key Steps in the Federal Hiring Process 144
- 17.2 Creating a USAJOBS Profile 145
  - 17.2.1 Setting Up Your USAJOBS Profile 145
  - 17.2.2 Setting Job Preferences 145
- 17.3 Writing an Effective Federal Resume 146
  - 17.3.2 Essential Sections for a Federal Resume 146
  - 17.3.3 Using the USAJOBS Resume Builder 147
- 17.4 Understanding Veterans' Preference and Military Spouse Hiring Preferences 147
  - 17.4.1 Veterans' Preference 147
  - 17.4.2 Military Spouse Preference 148
- 17.5 Preparing for the Interview and Beyond 148
  - 17.5.1 Understanding the Federal Interview Process 148

17.5.2 Preparing for the Interview 149

17.5.3 Handling Multiple Interviews 149

17.6 Navigating Background Checks and Security Clearances 149

17.6.1 Understanding Federal Background Checks 149

17.6.2 Obtaining a Security Clearance 150

17.7 Navigating Special Hiring Programs for Veterans and Military Spouses 150

17.7.1 Veterans Recruitment Appointment (VRA) 151

17.7.2 Veterans Employment Opportunities Act (VEOA) 151

17.7.4 Non-Competitive Hiring for Military Spouses 151

Chapter 18: Salary Negotiation in Federal Employment: Maximizing Your Compensation 152

18.1 Understanding the Federal Pay System 152

18.1.1 The General Schedule (GS) Pay Scale 152

18.1.2 Other Federal Pay Systems 153

18.2 Assessing Your Salary Level 153

18.2.1 Determining Your GS Grade 153

18.2.2 Understanding Steps and Locality Pay 153

18.3 Strategies for Negotiating Your Salary 154

18.3.1 Negotiating Your Step 154

18.3.2 Negotiating Relocation and Recruitment Incentives 154

18.4 Other Benefits to Consider 155

18.4.1 Retirement and Health Benefits 155

18.4.2 Paid Leave and Work-Life Balance 155

Chapter 19: Applying for Federal Employment Overseas: Opportunities and Strategies for Military Service Members, Veterans, Military Spouses, and Civilians 157

19.1 Understanding Overseas Federal Employment 157

19.1.1 Types of Overseas Federal Jobs 157

19.1.2 Locations and Agencies Offering Overseas Jobs 158

19.2 Navigating the Federal Hiring Process for Overseas Jobs 158

19.2.1 Using USAJOBS to Find Overseas Jobs 158

19.2.2 Understanding Eligibility and Hiring Preferences 159

19.2.3 Crafting an Overseas-Ready Federal Resume 159

19.3 Compensation and Benefits for Federal Employees Overseas 159

19.3.1 Overseas Pay Structures and Allowances 160

19.3.2 Tax Benefits and Exemptions 160

19.4 Preparing for Life and Work Abroad 160

19.4.1 Navigating the Relocation Process 160

19.4.2 Adapting to a New Culture 161

19.4.3 Managing Personal Well-Being Abroad 161

19.5 Leveraging Available Resources for Overseas Employees 162

19.5.1 Support from U.S. Embassies and Consulates 162

19.5.2 Military Base Support for Civilian Employees 162

19.6 Returning to the U.S. After an Overseas Assignment 163

19.6.1 Navigating Reassignment or Repatriation 163

19.6.2 Leveraging Overseas Experience for Career Advancement 163

Chapter 20: Understanding the Priority Placement Program (PPP) for Federal Employment 165

20.1 What is the Priority Placement Program (PPP)? 165

20.1.1 Purpose of the PPP 165

20.2 Eligibility for the Priority Placement Program 166

20.2.1 Categories of Eligible Employees 166

20.2.2 Criteria for Military Spouse Preference 166

20.2.3 Eligibility for Veterans and Wounded Warriors 166

20.3 How the Priority Placement Program Works 167

20.3.1 Registration in the Program 167

20.3.2 Job Matching and Placement Process 167

20.3.3 Military Spouse Employment Preferences (PPP-S) 168

20.4 Benefits of the Priority Placement Program 168

20.4.1 Job Security During Transition 168

20.4.2 Support for Military Spouses 168

20.4.3 Career Continuity 168

20.5 Tips for Maximizing the Benefits of PPP 169

20.5.1 Be Proactive in Registration 169

20.5.2 Be Flexible with Location and Roles 169

20.5.3 Stay Engaged with HR and Support Services 169

Chapter 1: Crafting the Perfect Resume

Your resume is often the first impression you'll make on a potential employer, so it's crucial to craft a resume that clearly communicates your skills, experience, and value. In this chapter, we'll walk through how to structure your resume, tailor it for specific job applications, and highlight your achievements in a way that catches the attention of hiring managers.

1.1 Understanding the Purpose of a Resume

A resume is not a complete biography

of your career. Rather, it's a marketing document that highlights your most relevant experience, skills, and accomplishments in relation to the specific job you're applying for. The goal of a resume is to get you an interview, not necessarily to get you the job. Therefore, you want your resume to be clear, concise, and tailored for each opportunity.

1.2 Resume Formats: Which One is Right for You?

There are three main types of resume formats: reverse-chronological, functional, and combination. Choosing the right format depends on your career history, the job you're applying for, and how you want to present your skills.

1.2.1 Reverse-Chronological Resume

This is the most common and widely accepted resume format. It lists your work experience in reverse order, starting with your most recent position. This format is ideal for those with a steady work history and clear career progression.

When to use it:
- You have a strong work history without significant gaps.
- You want to highlight your career growth.
- The job you're applying for is directly related to your previous positions.

Key sections:
- Contact Information
- Summary or Objective Statement
- Work Experience (listed in reverse-chronological order)
- Education
- Skills
- Certifications (if applicable)

1.2.2 Functional Resume

The functional resume focuses on your skills and abilities rather than your chronological work history. It's best for individuals with gaps in employment, those changing careers, or those with less conventional work experiences.

When to use it:
- You are shifting to a new industry or career.
- You have gaps in your work history.
- Your experience comes from various roles that don't align chronologically.

Key sections:
- Contact Information
- Skills Summary
- Relevant Skills and Accomplishments
- Work Experience (optional and often very brief)
- Education

1.2.3 Combination Resume

This format blends both the reverse-chronological and functional resumes. It focuses on your skills but also provides a detailed work history. It is useful for job seekers with a robust set of skills and accomplishments but who also want to show a clear work history.

When to use it:
- You want to emphasize skills while still showing your job progression.
- You have a diverse skill set and a solid work history.

Key sections:
- Contact Information
- Summary or Objective Statement
- Skills Summary
- Work Experience (in reverse-chronological order)
- Education
- Certifications (if applicable)

1.3 The Anatomy of a Great Resume

Now that you've selected the right format, let's break down each essential section of the resume and what to include.

1.3.1 Contact Information

This is the simplest but most crucial part of your resume. It should be at the very top of your document and must include:

- Full Name
- Phone Number
- Professional Email Address (avoid using personal or unprofessional emails)
- LinkedIn Profile (optional but recommended)
- Address (optional, can be city/state only)

Pro Tip: Ensure your email address is professional, such as firstname.lastname@email.com. Unprofessional email addresses can leave a negative impression.

1.3.2 Summary or Objective Statement

This is a short, concise paragraph that sums up your professional background, key skills, and career objectives.

A summary is ideal if you have significant experience and want to highlight your expertise.

Example: "Experienced project manager with 10+ years of leading cross-functional teams in delivering complex projects on time and under budget. Proven track record in risk management, process optimization, and team leadership."

An objective is suitable if you're at the beginning of your career or shifting industries.

Example: "Recent graduate with a degree in marketing, seeking to leverage communication skills and creative problem-solving in a role as a marketing coordinator."

Pro Tip: Customize your summary or objective for each job application to align with the company's needs and goals.

1.3.3 Work Experience

Your work experience is the heart of your resume, especially if you're using the reverse-chronological or combination formats. When listing your jobs, follow these guidelines:
- Start with your most recent position and work backward.
- Include the job title, company name, location, and dates of employment.
- Use bullet points to describe your responsibilities and achievements.
- Quantify your achievements where possible (e.g., "Increased sales by 20% over six months").
- Use action verbs to begin each bullet point (e.g., managed, developed, implemented, led).

Example:

Marketing Coordinator | ABC Company, New York, NY | June 2020 – Present
Developed and executed marketing campaigns that increased product sales by 15%.
Managed social media accounts, growing engagement by 30% within six months.

Collaborated with the design team to create promotional materials for major product launches.

> *Pro Tip: Focus on achievements, not just responsibilities. Employers want to see how you added value in your previous roles.*

1.3.4 Education

In this section, list your most recent and relevant educational achievements. Include:
- The degree obtained (e.g., Bachelor of Science in Marketing)
- The institution name and location
- Your graduation date
- Relevant coursework (optional, if you lack work experience or are changing fields)

If you've graduated within the last five years, you may also include your GPA, especially if it's over 3.5. However, omit this if it's been several years since you graduated or if your GPA is not particularly high.

1.3.5 Skills

List any relevant skills that align with the job you're applying for. Be specific and avoid generic terms like "good communicator" or "team player." Instead, focus on technical skills, languages, certifications, and industry-specific abilities.

Example:

Social Media Strategy
Google Analytics
Project Management (PMP Certified)
Adobe Creative Suite

1.4 Tailoring Your Resume to Each Job

One of the biggest mistakes job seekers make is sending the same resume to every employer. Tailoring your resume to fit the job description is crucial in making it through Applicant Tracking Systems (ATS) and catching the hiring manager's attention.

1.4.1 Analyze the Job Description

Start by closely reading the job description and noting the specific skills, qualifications, and experience required. Identify keywords and phrases that appear frequently.

1.4.2 Match Your Resume to the Job

Adjust your summary/objective to reflect the company's needs. Use the same keywords from the job posting in your resume, especially in the skills and experience sections. Highlight specific accomplishments that align with the job's responsibilities.

Pro Tip: Even small adjustments, like using the exact job title listed in the posting, can increase your chances of getting noticed.

1.5 The Importance of Formatting and Design

While content is king, the visual presentation of your resume is also critical. Follow these formatting best practices:
- Keep it clean and simple: Avoid overly complex designs or graphics. Stick to a professional, easy-to-read font (e.g., Arial, Calibri) in a size between 10 and 12 points.
- One page for most: Unless you have 10+ years of experience, aim to keep your resume to one page.
- Consistent formatting: Ensure uniformity in headings, fonts, and bullet points.
- White space is your friend: Avoid overcrowding your resume. Use margins and spacing to make it visually appealing.

1.6 Common Resume Mistakes to Avoid

To ensure your resume stands out for the right reasons, steer clear of these common mistakes:
- Spelling and grammatical errors: Proofread multiple times, and consider
- having someone else review it.
- Including irrelevant experience: Focus only on jobs and skills that relate to the position you're applying for.
- Using a one-size-fits-all resume: Always tailor your resume to each specific job.
- Overusing buzzwords: While it's important to match keywords, avoid clichés like "team player" or "hard worker" without backing them up with evidence.

Conclusion

A well-crafted resume is your ticket to getting noticed by employers. By selecting the right format, highlighting your most relevant accomplishments, and tailoring your resume to each job, you significantly increase your chances of landing an interview. Remember, the key to a standout resume is not just what you've done, but how you present it.

Chapter 2: Crafting a Cover Letter That Stands Out

While the resume provides a snapshot of your skills and experience, the cover letter gives you an opportunity to explain who you are, why you're a good fit for the position, and what you can bring to the company. This chapter will explore the structure of an effective cover letter, tips for customization, and common mistakes to avoid.

2.1 The Purpose of a Cover Letter

A cover letter is your chance to tell a story that your resume can't. It's where you can:
- Express enthusiasm for the role and company.
- Clarify how your experience makes you a strong fit for the job.
- Explain any unusual circumstances (such as employment gaps or career changes).
- Provide a personalized narrative that sets you apart from other candidates.

A well-written cover letter should complement, not duplicate, the information in your resume. It gives the hiring manager a sense of your personality and communication style, which can be particularly important for roles that require written communication skills.

2.2 Structuring Your Cover Letter

A great cover letter follows a clear and concise structure that includes an introduction, a few body paragraphs, and a conclusion. Let's break it down step by step.

2.2.1 Contact Information and Header

At the top of your cover letter, include your contact information (name, phone number, email) and the date. Below that, add the employer's contact information, including the hiring manager's name, their title, the company name, and the company's address.

Example:

Jane Doe
jane.doe@email.com
(123) 456-7890
[LinkedIn Profile (optional)]

October 1, 2024

Hiring Manager
ABC Company
123 Business St.
New York, NY 10001

2.2.2 Salutation

Whenever possible, address the cover letter to a specific person. This shows that you've done your research and are genuinely interested in the position. Avoid generic salutations like "To Whom It May Concern."

If the job posting lists the hiring manager's name, use it: "Dear Mr. Smith," or "Dear Ms. Johnson,".

If you can't find a name, you can use: "Dear Hiring Manager," or "Dear [Department] Team,".

> *Pro Tip: Be sure to use the correct titles and gender identifiers, or default to "Dear [Full Name]" if unsure.*

2.2.3 Introduction: Grab Their Attention

Your opening paragraph should be attention-grabbing and tailored to the specific job and company. Use this section to express your excitement for the role and explain how you learned about the opportunity.

In this paragraph:
- Mention the specific job title you're applying for.
- Show your enthusiasm for the role and the company.
- Briefly introduce your qualifications that align with the job.

Example:

"I was excited to come across the opening for the Marketing Coordinator position at ABC Company. With over five years of experience leading successful digital marketing campaigns and a passion for driving results through innovative strategies, I am confident that my skills align with the needs of your team."

> *Pro Tip: Avoid starting with "I am writing to apply for..." This is standard but boring. Instead, use this space to show your passion and excitement.*

2.2.4 Body: Connect Your Skills to the Job

In the body of the cover letter (typically 1-3 paragraphs), expand on how your experience makes you a great fit for the role. This is where you show the employer why they should be excited to interview you.

2.2.4.1 Demonstrating Your Qualifications

Use this section to directly tie your qualifications to the job description. Highlight relevant experience, skills, and accomplishments that align with the role you're applying for. Rather than rehashing your resume, provide context and tell stories that demonstrate your strengths.

For each job requirement or skill mentioned in the posting, offer a concrete example of how you've demonstrated that ability.

Example:

"In my previous role as a Marketing Specialist at XYZ Corp., I developed and executed a digital marketing campaign that resulted in a 20% increase in website traffic and a 15% boost in sales within six months. By collaborating with cross-functional teams and utilizing data-driven strategies, I ensured that the campaign reached target audiences and achieved measurable success."

2.2.4.2 Explaining Employment Gaps or Career Changes

If you have any employment gaps or are making a career change, use the cover letter to briefly explain your situation in a positive light. Focus on how your skills are transferable and how you'll bring value to the new role.

Example:

"After taking two years to care for a family member, I am eager to re-enter the workforce. During this time, I remained up to date on industry trends through online courses and freelance projects, ensuring that I am well-prepared to contribute to your team."

> *Pro Tip: Be honest, but don't dwell on negatives. Keep explanations short and focus on what you bring to the table.*

2.3 Customizing Your Cover Letter

A common mistake is to send out the same cover letter to every employer. Customization is key to making a strong impression and standing out from other applicants.

2.3.1 Research the Company

Before you write the cover letter, do your research on the company. Understanding the company's mission, values, and culture can help you tailor your message.

- Check the company's website, social media, and recent news.
- Identify what makes this company different from others in the industry.

- Look for specific challenges the company is facing, and mention how your skills could help address those challenges.

Example:

"I am particularly drawn to ABC Company's commitment to sustainability and innovation. As someone who is passionate about environmentally conscious marketing, I would love the opportunity to contribute to your ongoing efforts to reduce the company's carbon footprint."

2.3.2 Reflect the Job Description

- Customize your cover letter to reflect the exact job description. Echo the key skills and qualifications mentioned in the posting and address them in your letter.
- If the job description emphasizes teamwork, mention your experience working in teams.
- If the company is looking for a problem-solver, share an example of how you've solved a complex issue.

Pro Tip: While it's important to use keywords from the job description, avoid simply copying and pasting the job requirements. Weave them naturally into your narrative.

2.4 Conclusion: Closing with a Call to Action

Your closing paragraph should:
- Reiterate your enthusiasm for the role and the company.
- Highlight how your skills align with the company's goals.
- Express your desire to discuss your application in further detail.
- Politely suggest the next step (usually an interview).

Example:

"I am excited about the opportunity to bring my skills and experience in digital marketing to the ABC Company team. I would welcome the chance to further discuss how my background can contribute to your marketing efforts. Thank you for considering my application, and I look forward to the possibility of working together."

Pro Tip: Keep your closing polite but assertive. You want to demonstrate your eagerness without being pushy.

2.5 Common Mistakes to Avoid

Writing a cover letter is an art, and there are common pitfalls you'll want to avoid:

2.5.1 Generic Language

Avoid using the same tired phrases that everyone else is using. Be specific and thoughtful in how you describe your experience and passion.

Instead of: "I am a hard worker and a team player."

Try: "I thrive in collaborative environments and have successfully led cross-functional teams to deliver high-impact projects."

2.5.2 Restating Your Resume

Your cover letter should complement your resume, not repeat it. Use this space to provide additional insights into your experience and personality.

2.5.3 Focusing on What You Want

A common mistake is focusing too much on what you're looking for in a job. While it's okay to mention why you're excited about the role, your main focus should be on how you can help the company.

2.5.4 Being Too Long or Too Short

Aim for a cover letter that's roughly three to four paragraphs long and no more than one page. Keep it concise but informative.

2.6 Proofreading and Finalizing Your Cover Letter

Your cover letter is often the first impression you make, so it needs to be error-free. Follow these steps to ensure it's polished:

2.6.1 Proofread Multiple Times

Look for spelling errors, grammar mistakes, and awkward phrasing. Consider reading it out loud to catch issues you might miss when reading silently.

2.6.2 Get a Second Opinion

If possible, ask a friend, mentor, or colleague to review your cover letter. A fresh pair of eyes can often catch things you might miss.

2.6.3 Ensure Consistency with Your Resume

Your cover letter should match your resume in terms of tone, style, and formatting. Use the same font and formatting style to ensure your application package looks professional.

Conclusion

A well-crafted cover letter can be the key to getting your foot in the door. By demonstrating your enthusiasm, clearly connecting your experience to the job, and customizing your letter for each application, you can greatly increase your chances of standing out from the crowd. Remember, this is your chance to tell a compelling story that a resume alone cannot capture.

2.7 How to Handle Different Types of Cover Letters

Not all job applications are the same. Some require traditional cover letters, while others may ask for more specific or unique approaches. Here's how to handle various situations:

2.7.1 Applying for a Job Online

Many online job applications require you to submit a cover letter as part of an automated system. In these cases:

- Ensure your cover letter is formatted for easy readability. Avoid complicated layouts since some applicant tracking systems (ATS) may strip out formatting.
- Focus heavily on including keywords from the job description to help your application make it through ATS filters.
- If possible, upload your cover letter as a PDF to preserve formatting and ensure that it looks professional across all devices.

Pro Tip: If there's a field for a "cover letter" but no specific instruction to upload one, still take the time to write a brief cover letter in the field provided. It can give you an edge over candidates who skip it.

2.7.2 Cold Outreach or Unadvertised Jobs

Sometimes, you may want to apply to a company that hasn't posted any open positions. This requires a slightly different approach, as your goal is to convince the employer that they need you even if they weren't planning on hiring.

- Start by emphasizing your admiration for the company and what specifically draws you to them.
- Highlight your most valuable skills and how they could solve a potential problem for the company.
- Keep the letter concise and focus on how you can add value.

Example:

"I am reaching out to express my interest in potential opportunities with

ABC Company. As a data analyst with five years of experience optimizing business processes and enhancing data-driven decision-making, I am impressed by your company's commitment to using innovative strategies to stay ahead in the industry. I would love the opportunity to contribute to ABC's continued success."

Pro Tip: If you know someone who works at the company or have a connection, mention their name (with permission) to help make your letter stand out even more.

2.7.3 Internal Job Applications

If you're applying for a position within your current organization, your cover letter should:

- Emphasize your loyalty and dedication to the company.
- Highlight your accomplishments in your current role.
- Demonstrate your understanding of the company's culture and goals.

Example:

"As a member of the sales team for the past three years, I've had the opportunity to contribute to significant growth in revenue while building strong relationships with clients. I'm excited about the opportunity to transition into a management role and leverage my experience to drive continued success for ABC Company."

Pro Tip: While you're already familiar with the company, don't skip the research phase. Internal applicants are often held to higher standards, so ensure that you're fully prepared.

2.7.4 Applying to Startups or Creative Industries

Startups and creative industries often prefer a more casual, innovative approach to cover letters. While the basic structure should remain the same, you can inject a little more personality and creativity into your writing.

- Show passion and excitement about the company's mission.
- Use an engaging, conversational tone.
- Mention how your skills can help the company grow or tackle challenges unique to their industry.

Example:

"ABC Startup's commitment to revolutionizing sustainable energy is something I'm deeply passionate about. As a project manager with a background in renewable energy solutions, I thrive in fast-paced, dynamic environments like yours. I'm confident that my ability to lead cross-functional teams and drive innovative projects can help ABC Startup continue to disrupt the industry."

Pro Tip: While a more creative approach can work well in these industries, avoid being overly casual. Ensure your letter remains professional and focused on the value you bring.

2.7.5 When There's No Requirement for a Cover Letter

If a job application doesn't specifically ask for a cover letter, it can still be beneficial to include one. Many employers appreciate the extra effort, and it gives you another opportunity to sell yourself.

Pro Tip: Keep the letter brief, but still customize it for the role. A short, tailored cover letter can help you stand out even when it's not a requirement.

2.8 Tailoring for Specific Industries

Every industry has its own nuances, and tailoring your cover letter to match those expectations is essential.

2.8.1 Technology and Engineering

For technology and engineering roles, employers typically value hard skills and technical expertise. In your cover letter:

- Emphasize specific technical skills or certifications that match the job description.
- Provide examples of how you've applied these skills in previous roles.
- Use concise language and avoid unnecessary fluff.

Example:

"As a software engineer with 7 years of experience in developing scalable web applications, I am excited about the opportunity to join ABC Tech. My expertise in JavaScript frameworks, combined with my experience in Agile development environments, positions me to contribute to the success of your engineering team."

2.8.2 Healthcare

Healthcare roles often require a blend of technical expertise and compassion. Your cover letter should:
- Highlight relevant certifications, licenses, and experience.
- Emphasize your patient care or support skills.
- Show your passion for improving the well-being of others.

Example:

"As a registered nurse with 10 years of experience in critical care settings, I am passionate about providing high-quality, compassionate care to my patients. I have a strong track record of successfully managing patient treatment plans and collaborating with multidisciplinary teams to ensure the best possible outcomes."

2.8.3 Sales and Marketing

Sales and marketing cover letters should focus on results and metrics. Employers want to see proof that you can drive revenue or increase engagement, so:
- Emphasize your accomplishments and use numbers where possible.
- Showcase your communication and persuasion skills.
- Demonstrate your knowledge of current marketing trends or sales strategies.

Example:

"In my role as a Sales Manager at XYZ Corp., I consistently exceeded quarterly sales targets, growing revenue by 25% year over year. My experience building strong client relationships and leading successful sales teams would be an asset to ABC Company."

2.9 Leveraging Technology in Your Cover Letter

In the digital age, there are several ways to enhance your cover letter beyond simple text. Here are a few creative approaches to help you stand out:

2.9.1 Including Hyperlinks

If you have an online portfolio, LinkedIn profile, or relevant work samples, consider including hyperlinks in your cover letter.

Example:

"I have successfully managed marketing campaigns that resulted in a 30% increase in website traffic. You can view some of my recent work here [Insert hyperlink to portfolio]."

2.9.2 Incorporating Digital Media

For roles in design, media, or creative industries, you might consider linking to video introductions or multimedia projects. This shows your ability to think outside the box and use technology creatively.

Pro Tip: Make sure all links are working and lead to professional, relevant content.

Conclusion

A well-crafted cover letter can be your secret weapon in the job search process. It's your opportunity to connect your skills and experiences directly to the employer's needs, showcase your personality, and explain why you're the perfect fit for the role. By tailoring each letter, demonstrating your qualifications with concrete examples, and avoiding common pitfalls, you can significantly boost your chances of landing an interview. As with your resume, the key is to present yourself as a solution to the employer's challenges while making a lasting impression.

Chapter 3: Job Search Strategies: Navigating the Modern Job Market

The job search process has evolved significantly in recent years, with new tools, platforms, and strategies available to help you find the right position. However, knowing where and how to look for jobs can still be overwhelming. In this chapter, we'll cover various job search strategies, including how to leverage online platforms, build and utilize your professional network, and effectively apply for roles.

3.1 The Importance of a Targeted Job Search

Before diving into specific job search strategies, it's essential to understand why a targeted job search is far more effective than applying to as many positions as possible. A focused approach ensures you're applying to roles that align with your skills, experience, and interests, giving you a better chance of success.

3.1.1 Identify Your Career Goals

Take the time to reflect on your career goals before launching your job search. Ask yourself:
- What are my short-term and long-term career objectives?
- What type of work environment suits me best (e.g., remote, hybrid, office-based)?
- What industries or companies am I most interested in?
- What job titles and roles fit my skill set?

Once you have clarity on your goals, you can begin targeting roles that match your ambitions.

3.1.2 Research Potential Employers

A key part of a targeted job search is researching companies that align with your values, culture preferences, and goals. Investigate a company's:
- Mission and values.
- Industry reputation and stability.
- Workplace culture.
- Opportunities for growth and development.
- Commitment to diversity and inclusion.

Researching potential employers not only helps you find the right job but also equips you with valuable information to use during interviews.

3.2 Leveraging Job Boards and Online Platforms

The internet offers an array of tools and platforms to help you search for jobs more efficiently. Let's break down some of the most effective online job search platforms and how to use them.

3.2.1 General Job Boards

Job boards are websites where companies post available positions, and candidates can apply. Many general job boards cover multiple industries, job types, and levels of experience.

Popular General Job Boards:
- Indeed: One of the largest job search engines, it aggregates listings from across the web. Use the filters to search by location, salary, experience level, and more.
- LinkedIn Jobs: In addition to its networking features, LinkedIn also offers a robust job search engine. LinkedIn lets you see how you are connected to people at companies that are hiring, providing an opportunity for a warm introduction.
- Glassdoor: Glassdoor allows you to search for jobs and see company reviews, salary data, and interview insights, making it an excellent resource for researching potential employers.
- Monster: A longstanding job board that offers a variety of tools for both job seekers and employers.
- Pro Tip: Set up job alerts on these platforms to receive notifications when positions that match your criteria become available.

3.2.2 Niche Job Boards

In addition to general job boards, consider using niche platforms that cater to specific industries, professions, or job types. These boards often feature jobs that are not posted on larger platforms and can provide opportunities more tailored to your field.

Examples of Niche Job Boards:
- Dice: Focused on technology and IT roles.
- Idealist: Specializes in jobs for nonprofits and mission-driven organizations.
- Mediabistro: Targeted at media, communications, and creative professionals.
- FlexJobs: Lists remote, part-time, freelance, and flexible job opportunities.
- VetJobs: Dedicated to job opportunities for veterans and transitioning service members.

3.2.3 Company Websites

Some companies post job listings only on their own websites, particularly if they're large organizations with frequent openings. If there are specific companies you're interested in working for, visit their careers page directly.

Pro Tip: Bookmark the career pages of your top companies and check them regularly or set alerts through platforms like LinkedIn or Google Alerts.

3.2.4 Aggregators

Job search aggregators pull job listings from various sources, including company websites and job boards, into one place. This can save time by providing a one-stop-shop for job postings.

Popular Aggregators:
- SimplyHired
- CareerBuilder
- ZipRecruiter

3.3 Maximizing LinkedIn for Job Search Success

LinkedIn is one of the most powerful tools for job seekers. Not only can you search for jobs, but you can also use it to build your network, showcase your expertise, and get noticed by recruiters.

3.3.1 Optimizing Your LinkedIn Profile

Your LinkedIn profile is your online professional presence, so it's essential to keep it updated and optimized. Here's how to ensure your profile stands out:
- Professional Photo: Use a high-quality, professional headshot.
- Compelling Headline: Your headline is one of the first things people see. Instead of just listing your current job title, make it a concise summary of who you are professionally (e.g., "Experienced Marketing Manager | Specializing in Digital Strategies and Brand Growth").
- Detailed Summary: Use the summary section to tell your professional story. Highlight your skills, experience, and career goals. Be sure to include relevant keywords.
- Experience Section: Just like your resume, your experience section should focus on your accomplishments and results. Use bullet points and quantify your achievements where possible.
- Skills and Endorsements: List your key skills, and ask colleagues to endorse you for them. This boosts your profile's credibility.
- Recommendations: Request recommendations from past managers, colleagues, or clients. These can serve as testimonials of your work ethic and abilities.

Pro Tip: Engage with LinkedIn regularly. Share articles, comment on industry-related posts, and connect with others in your field.

3.3.2 Using LinkedIn Jobs

LinkedIn's job search feature allows you to:
- Search for jobs based on keywords, location, industry, and more.

- Filter jobs by experience level, company size, and remote work options.
- See how you are connected to people at the hiring company.
- Set job alerts to receive notifications about new listings that match your criteria.

Additionally, LinkedIn offers an "Easy Apply" feature for some listings, allowing you to apply quickly using your profile information.

3.3.3 Engaging with Recruiters and Networking on LinkedIn

LinkedIn also allows you to connect directly with recruiters and hiring managers. When sending a connection request, include a personalized message introducing yourself and explaining your interest.

Example Message:

"Hi [Name], I noticed that you are the hiring manager for [Position] at [Company]. I am very interested in applying and would love to connect to learn more about the role. Thank you for your time!"

Pro Tip: Use LinkedIn's "Open to Work" feature to let recruiters know you're open to job opportunities. This can help you appear in more recruiter searches.

3.4 Networking: The Key to Hidden Job Opportunities

Networking is one of the most effective ways to find job opportunities, many of which are never advertised. Building and maintaining a strong professional network can open doors to new roles and lead to referrals.

3.4.1 Expanding Your Network

Building a diverse network takes time but is highly rewarding. You can expand your professional connections by:
- Attending industry conferences, workshops, or job fairs.
- Joining professional associations or networking groups.
- Engaging with alumni networks from your university.
- Participating in online forums, webinars, or LinkedIn groups.

3.4.2 Reaching Out to Your Existing Network

Your existing network of friends, family, former colleagues, and mentors can also be a great resource. Let them know that you're in the job market and ask if they can keep an eye out for opportunities or provide introductions.

Example Message:

"Hi [Name], I hope you're doing well. I wanted to reach out because I'm currently exploring new opportunities in [Industry/Field]. If you hear of any roles that might be a good fit, I would greatly appreciate a referral or introduction. Thank you!"

3.4.3 Informational Interviews

An informational interview is a great way to learn more about a particular industry, company, or role. It's not about asking for a job, but rather gathering valuable insights that could help you in your search.

To set up an informational interview, reach out to someone in your network or a connection on LinkedIn, and politely ask for a few minutes of their time to discuss their career path or industry insights.

Example Request:

"Dear [Name], I admire the work you've done in [Industry/Field] and would love the opportunity to learn more about your career journey. I'm currently exploring opportunities in this area and was wondering if you might have time for a brief chat. Thank you for considering my request."

3.5 Job Fairs and Networking Events

Job fairs and networking events provide direct access to employers and recruiters, making them a valuable part of your job search strategy. These events may be industry-specific or general, and they can be held virtually or in person.

3.5.1 How to Prepare for a Job Fair

Research the Attending Companies: Review the list of companies that will be at the event, and prioritize those you're most interested in.

Prepare Your Elevator Pitch: Be ready to introduce yourself, explain what you do, and express your interest in the company or role in a brief, engaging way.

Bring Copies of Your Resume: Always have printed copies of your resume on hand, even if it's a virtual job fair where you may need to submit it digitally. Make sure it's tailored to the types of roles you're interested in.

3.5.2 Maximizing Your Time at a Job Fair

Prioritize Your Top Companies: Begin by visiting the companies you're most interested in. Time can be limited at large fairs, so focus on the employers that align with your goals first.

Engage with Recruiters: Ask thoughtful questions about the company and available roles. Show genuine interest and enthusiasm.

Take Notes: After speaking with a recruiter, jot down a few key points from the conversation. This will help you follow up later with personalized messages or emails.

3.5.3 Following Up After a Job Fair

Following up after a job fair is crucial. It reinforces your interest and helps you stand out from other candidates. Send a polite, professional thank-you note or email within 24 to 48 hours of the event.

Example Follow-Up Email:

"Dear [Recruiter's Name],

Thank you for taking the time to speak with me at [Job Fair Name]. I enjoyed learning more about the opportunities at [Company Name] and am excited about the possibility of contributing to your team. I believe my experience in [Relevant Field/Skill] would be a great fit for [Position Title].

I've attached my resume for your reference and look forward to discussing how my skills align with the company's goals. Thank you again for your time, and I hope to stay in touch!

Best regards,
[Your Name]"

3.6 Cold Outreach and Direct Applications

While most people focus on applying to posted job openings, cold outreach can be a powerful way to uncover hidden opportunities, especially in smaller companies or startups.

3.6.1 What is Cold Outreach?

Cold outreach involves reaching out to companies that aren't actively advertising a position but could still have a need for someone with your skills. This approach is more proactive and can sometimes result in jobs being created specifically for you.

3.6.2 How to Write a Cold Outreach Email

In a cold outreach email, the goal is to express interest in the company, showcase how your skills align with their needs, and open a line of communication. Be concise and focused on what value you can bring to the organization.

Example Cold Outreach Email:

"Dear [Hiring Manager's Name],

I'm writing to express my interest in potential opportunities at [Company Name]. With over [X years] of experience in [Your Industry/Field], I've developed a strong skill set in [specific skill or achievement]. I admire [Company Name]'s work in [specific project, mission, or value], and I would love the chance to contribute to your team.

I've attached my resume for your consideration and would appreciate the opportunity to discuss how my skills could benefit [Company Name]. Thank you for your time, and I look forward to hearing from you.

Best regards,
[Your Name]"

Pro Tip: Customize each cold outreach email. Mention specific projects or achievements by the company and explain why you're interested in contributing to their work.

3.7 Standing Out in a Competitive Job Market

In competitive job markets, simply applying to job postings isn't always enough. You'll need to be strategic and proactive to stand out from other candidates. Here are some advanced techniques to help you rise above the competition:

3.7.1 Building a Personal Brand

Your personal brand is how you present yourself to employers both online and in person. It's the combination of your skills, experience, values, and professional reputation.

Create a Professional Website or Portfolio: A personal website can showcase your work, projects, and accomplishments in more detail than a resume. It's particularly valuable in creative fields, but professionals in any industry can benefit from having an online presence.

Write Thought Leadership Articles: If you're an expert in your field, consider writing articles or blog posts on platforms like LinkedIn or Medium. Sharing your knowledge can help position you as a thought leader and attract attention from recruiters.

Engage with Industry Communities: Join online forums or LinkedIn groups relevant to your field. Participate in discussions, answer questions, and share valuable resources. Being active in your professional community can lead to networking opportunities and job leads.

3.7.2 Volunteering or Freelancing

If you're struggling to find full-time employment, consider volunteering or taking on freelance projects to keep your skills sharp and expand your network.

Volunteer Work: Look for opportunities to volunteer with nonprofit organizations or community groups in your field. This can help you gain experience, build connections, and even lead to full-time job offers.

Freelancing: Platforms like Upwork, Fiverr, and Freelancer offer a wide range of freelance opportunities. This is particularly useful for professionals in marketing, writing, design, programming, and consulting.

3.7.3 Get Certified or Take Courses

Continuing your education is a great way to stand out in a competitive job market. Many industries have certifications that can enhance your resume and make you more attractive to employers.

Online Learning Platforms: Websites like Coursera, LinkedIn Learning, and Udemy offer a wide range of courses that can help you develop new skills.

Industry-Specific Certifications: Research the certifications that are most valued in your industry, and consider pursuing one to boost your qualifications.

3.8 Tracking Your Job Applications

As you apply to multiple jobs, it's important to stay organized. Keeping track of your applications helps you follow up appropriately and ensures that you don't miss any deadlines.

3.8.1 Create a Job Application Tracker

You can use a simple spreadsheet or an online tool to track your job applications. Include the following columns:
- Company Name
- Job Title
- Date Applied
- Application Status (e.g., Applied, Interviewing, Offer Received)
- Contact Information (for the hiring manager or recruiter)
- Follow-Up Dates (when you plan to follow up)

3.8.2 Follow-Up on Applications

Following up on your applications can help keep your name top of mind with recruiters. After applying, wait about one to two weeks before sending a polite follow-up email to check on the status of your application.

Example Follow-Up Email:

"Dear [Hiring Manager's Name],

I hope this message finds you well. I wanted to follow up on my application for the [Position Title] role at [Company Name]. I remain very interested in the opportunity and would love to learn more about the next steps in the process. Thank you for considering my application, and I look forward to hearing from you soon.

Best regards,
[Your Name]"

Conclusion

The job search process can be overwhelming, but with the right strategies and tools, you can maximize your chances of landing the perfect role. By leveraging job boards, optimizing your LinkedIn profile, expanding your professional network, and using proactive outreach methods, you'll be well-equipped to navigate the modern job market. Remember, persistence and organization are key. Stay focused, track your progress, and be open to exploring new opportunities, and soon enough, you'll find yourself in a position that aligns with your skills, goals, and aspirations.

Chapter 4: Interviewing with Confidence: Mastering the Art of the Job Interview

The job interview is often the most crucial part of the job search process. It's your chance to show potential employers not only that you are qualified for the role but also that you are the right fit for the company. In this chapter, we'll cover everything you need to know to prepare for interviews, from researching the company to answering tough questions and following up after the interview.

4.1 Preparing for the Interview

Preparation is key to interviewing with confidence. The more prepared you are, the more comfortable and polished you will be during the interview. Let's break down the steps for thorough preparation.

4.1.1 Research the Company

Understanding the company is essential to making a good impression. Your research should go beyond just knowing the company's products or services. You should also familiarize yourself with the company's culture, mission, and recent developments.

Key Areas to Research:
- Company History and Mission: Understand the company's goals, values, and long-term vision.
- Products, Services, or Projects: Know what the company does or what it sells. If applicable, review their current projects or recent initiatives.
- Industry Trends: Be aware of the challenges and opportunities facing the industry in which the company operates.
- Company Culture: Look for clues about the company's culture through its website, social media, employee reviews (on platforms like Glassdoor), and LinkedIn profiles of current employees.

Pro Tip: If you can reference something specific about the company during the interview—like a recent project or a shared value—it shows the interviewer that you've done your homework and are genuinely interested in the role.

4.1.2 Review the Job Description

The job description is your guide to what the employer is looking for. Review it carefully and identify the key qualifications and responsibilities of the role. You should be able to explain how your skills and experience match those needs.

Key Questions to Ask Yourself:
- What are the core skills and qualifications listed?
- How do my past experiences align with the job responsibilities?

- What specific examples can I provide that demonstrate my ability to perform in this role?

Pro Tip: Print out the job description or have it readily accessible during your preparation. This allows you to tailor your answers and highlight the skills that the employer values most.

4.1.3 Prepare Your Responses to Common Interview Questions

While you can't predict every question, certain interview questions are almost guaranteed to come up. Preparing answers in advance will help you feel more confident and articulate during the interview.

Common Interview Questions:

- Tell me about yourself: This is often an icebreaker, but it sets the tone for the rest of the interview. Focus on a concise summary of your background, highlighting relevant experience and why you're excited about the opportunity.

- Why do you want to work here?: Show that you've researched the company and explain why its mission, culture, or the specific role aligns with your goals and values.

- What are your strengths and weaknesses?: Focus on strengths that are relevant to the job. When discussing weaknesses, choose one that you're actively working to improve.

- Tell me about a time when you…: Behavioral questions often begin with "Tell me about a time when…" and are designed to assess how you handle various situations. Use the STAR method (Situation, Task, Action, Result) to structure your answers.

- Where do you see yourself in five years?: Employers want to gauge your long-term commitment and ambitions. Your answer should reflect your interest in growth and how the role fits into your career plan.

4.2 The STAR Method: Answering Behavioral Questions

Behavioral interview questions are designed to assess how you've handled situations in the past because they can indicate how you'll perform in the future. To answer these effectively, use the STAR Method:

1. Situation: Describe the context or background of the situation.
2. Task: Explain the task you were responsible for or the challenge you faced.
3. Action: Detail the specific steps you took to address the situation.
4. Result: Share the outcome or results of your actions, quantifying them if possible (e.g., improved sales by 15%).

Example Question: "Tell me about a time when you had to deal with a difficult client."

STAR Answer:

Situation: "At my previous job as a customer service representative, we had a client who was very upset because their order had been delayed."

Task: "My responsibility was to calm the client down and resolve the issue while maintaining a positive relationship."

Action: "I first listened to their concerns and apologized for the delay. Then, I expedited the order and offered a discount on their next purchase as a goodwill gesture."

Result: "The client appreciated the resolution, and not only did we retain their business, but they also referred us to several other customers."

Pro Tip: Practice answering a variety of behavioral questions using the STAR method to get comfortable with the structure.

4.3 Preparing Questions for the Interviewer

At the end of most interviews, you'll be asked, "Do you have any questions for us?" This is your chance to learn more about the role and demonstrate your interest in the company. Prepare a list of insightful questions in advance.

Sample Questions to Ask:
- "What does a typical day look like for someone in this position?"
- "How do you measure success in this role?"
- "Can you tell me more about the team I'll be working with?"
- "What are the company's biggest challenges right now?"
- "How would you describe the company culture?"
- "Do you have any hesitation in hiring me?"

Pro Tip: Avoid asking questions that can easily be answered by looking at the company's website, such as basic information about the company's products or services. Instead, focus on asking questions that show you're thinking deeply about the role and how you can contribute.

4.4 The Day of the Interview: Making a Great First Impression

First impressions are critical, and they begin the moment you arrive — whether your interview is in-person or virtual. Here's how to prepare for a smooth and professional interview day.

4.4.1 Dress Appropriately

Your appearance sets the tone for how you'll be perceived. The general rule is to dress slightly more formally than the company's usual dress code. If you're unsure of what to wear, business professional attire (e.g., a suit or a tailored dress) is usually a safe choice.

In-Person Interviews: Dress neatly and conservatively. Ensure your clothes are clean, ironed, and appropriate for the company's culture.

Virtual Interviews: Even though the interview is online, dress professionally from head to toe. This ensures you feel fully prepared and prevents any embarrassment if you need to stand up during the call.

4.4.2 Arrive on Time

Punctuality is crucial. Aim to arrive at the interview location (or log into the virtual meeting) 10 to 15 minutes early. If it's an in-person interview, give yourself plenty of time to account for traffic, parking, or public transportation delays.

In-Person Interviews: Plan your route in advance and do a trial run if possible to ensure you know exactly how to get there.

Virtual Interviews: Test your technology ahead of time. Make sure your computer, microphone, and camera are working, and ensure that your internet connection is stable.

4.4.3 Bring the Necessary Materials

For in-person interviews, bring extra copies of your resume, a list of references, a notepad, and a pen. It's also a good idea to have a portfolio or examples of your work if applicable.

For virtual interviews, have a digital version of your resume and any other relevant documents easily accessible on your computer. You may also want to keep a notepad nearby to jot down any important points.

4.4.4 Nonverbal Communication

Your body language during the interview can say just as much as your words. Maintain eye contact, smile when appropriate, and sit up straight. Avoid crossing your arms or fidgeting, as this can make you appear nervous or defensive.

> *Pro Tip: Practice shaking hands firmly but not too aggressively. A weak handshake can leave a negative impression, while an overly firm handshake may come off as aggressive.*

4.5 Handling Different Types of Interviews

Interviews come in many forms, and it's important to be prepared for any format you might encounter.

4.5.1 Phone Interviews

Phone interviews are often the first step in the hiring process and are used to screen candidates before a more in-depth interview.

Tips for Success:
- Find a quiet place where you won't be interrupted.
- Smile while you speak—it can actually make your voice sound more positive and engaging.
- Have your resume and the job description in front of you for reference.
- Listen carefully and speak clearly. Since there are no visual cues, it's important to articulate your points well.

4.5.2 Video Interviews

Video interviews are becoming more common, especially in remote work environments. Treat a video interview just like an in-person interview, but with a few extra considerations.

Tips for Success:
- Test your camera and microphone beforehand to ensure everything works properly.
- Choose a clean, professional background and make sure your space is well-lit.
- Look directly at the camera when speaking to maintain eye contact with the interviewer.

4.5.3 Panel Interviews

In a panel interview, you'll meet with multiple interviewers at the same time. This can be intimidating, but with preparation, you can handle it confidently.

Tips for Success:
- Address Everyone: Make sure to engage with each interviewer, even if one person is asking most of the questions. Make eye contact and direct your responses to the group.
- Stay Calm and Composed: Panel interviews can feel overwhelming because multiple people are assessing you at once. Stay calm, listen carefully to each question, and take your time to answer thoughtfully.
- Prepare for Different Perspectives: In a panel interview, you may be interviewed by individuals from different departments. Be prepared to answer questions from

multiple perspectives (e.g., a technical expert might ask about your skills, while an HR professional might focus on culture fit).

4.5.4 Group Interviews

In a group interview, you will be interviewed alongside other candidates. This format is often used to assess how well candidates collaborate, communicate, and perform under pressure.

Tips for Success:
- Stand Out, But Don't Dominate: It's important to contribute to the discussion, but don't try to outshine or overshadow other candidates. Show that you can work well in a team by listening, responding thoughtfully, and contributing valuable insights.
- Support Others: Group interviews are an opportunity to demonstrate leadership and teamwork. Acknowledge others' contributions, build on their ideas, and show that you're a collaborative team player.

4.5.5 Case or Problem-Solving Interviews

In some industries, particularly consulting, finance, and tech, you may encounter case interviews or problem-solving exercises where you're asked to work through a business problem or technical challenge in real-time.

Tips for Success:
- Clarify the Problem: If you're not clear on the problem, ask questions to ensure you understand the task. Clarification can prevent costly mistakes and shows that you're thoughtful in your approach.
- Think Out Loud: Interviewers want to understand your thought process, so explain your reasoning as you work through the problem. Even if you don't arrive at the perfect solution, demonstrating a logical approach is often just as important.
- Stay Calm Under Pressure: These types of interviews are designed to see how you handle stress. Even if the problem is difficult, remain composed and keep working through the solution step by step.

4.6 How to Handle Tough Interview Questions

Almost every interview will include a few tough questions designed to assess your problem-solving abilities, emotional intelligence, or ability to handle challenges. Here are some common tough questions and tips for answering them.

4.6.1 "What is your greatest weakness?"

This question is tricky because you don't want to disqualify yourself by mentioning a major flaw, but you also don't want to come off as insincere by saying something like, "I'm too much of a perfectionist."

How to Answer:
- Choose a Real Weakness: Pick a weakness that is real but not critical to the role, such as a skill you're actively working on improving.
- Explain How You're Working on It: Follow up by explaining what steps you're taking to improve that weakness.

Example: "One area I'm working on is public speaking. In the past, I've felt nervous when presenting to large groups. To improve, I've taken a public speaking course and started volunteering to lead presentations in my current role. I've already noticed significant improvements and feel much more confident in front of an audience."

4.6.2 "Why did you leave your last job?"

If you left your previous job under difficult circumstances, this question can feel uncomfortable. However, it's important to remain positive and professional in your response.

How to Answer:
- Be Honest but Positive: If you left for reasons like downsizing, career growth, or personal development, be straightforward. Avoid criticizing your former employer.
- Focus on the Future: Emphasize your desire for new challenges and growth opportunities.

Example: "After three years in my previous role, I felt that I had grown as much as I could within the company. I'm looking for a position where I can continue to develop my skills and take on new challenges, which is why I'm so excited about this opportunity with your company."

4.6.3 "Tell me about a time you failed."

Employers ask this question to see how you handle adversity, learn from mistakes, and demonstrate resilience.

How to Answer:
- Choose a Real Example: Select a failure that you genuinely learned from, but don't choose something catastrophic that might raise red flags.
- Focus on Growth: Explain what you learned from the experience and how it helped you grow professionally.

Example: "In my previous role, I led a project that didn't meet the client's expectations due to a miscommunication about their goals. While the project was completed, it didn't have the impact we'd hoped for. I took this as a learning experience and have since implemented stronger communication practices with clients to ensure that all expectations are clear before moving forward."

4.7 What to Do After the Interview: Following Up

The interview doesn't end when you walk out the door or log off the video call. Following up with the interviewer is a critical part of the process that can leave a lasting positive impression.

4.7.1 Send a Thank-You Email

A thoughtful thank-you email shows professionalism, reinforces your interest in the position, and gives you a chance to reiterate why you're the right fit for the role. Send the email within 24 hours of the interview.

What to Include:
- Thank the interviewer for their time.
- Mention something specific from the interview (e.g., a topic you discussed or an aspect of the company that excites you).
- Reiterate your enthusiasm for the role and how you can contribute.

Example:

Subject Line: Thank You – [Your Name], Interview for [Position]

Email Body: "Dear [Interviewer's Name],

Thank you so much for taking the time to meet with me today. I enjoyed our conversation about [specific topic discussed], and I'm even more excited about the opportunity to contribute to [Company Name] as a [Position Title].

I'm confident that my experience in [relevant skill/industry] and my passion

for [specific aspect of the company's work] would allow me to make a meaningful impact on your team. Please don't hesitate to reach out if you have any further questions, and I look forward to hearing from you soon.

Best regards,
[Your Name]"

4.7.2 Following Up on the Status of Your Application

If you haven't heard back after one to two weeks, it's appropriate to send a polite follow-up email inquiring about the status of your application.

Example Follow-Up Email:

Subject Line: Follow-Up on [Position] Interview

Email Body: "Dear [Interviewer's Name],

I hope you're doing well. I wanted to follow up on the status of my application for the [Position Title] role. I'm still very interested in the opportunity and would appreciate any updates on the next steps in the hiring process. Thank you for considering my application, and I look forward to hearing from you.

Best regards,
[Your Name]"

Conclusion

Mastering the interview process is about preparation, confidence, and professionalism. By researching the company, practicing common questions, using the STAR method for behavioral questions, and making a strong first impression, you'll be well-equipped to succeed. Remember, the interview is not just about proving your qualifications; it's about showing why you're the best fit for the role and the company. After the interview, following up with a thank-you email and maintaining professionalism throughout the process will reinforce your commitment and leave a lasting impression on the hiring team.

Chapter 5: The Follow-Up: Navigating Post-Interview Communication and Offers

Following up after an interview is an essential part of the job search process, but it's often overlooked. Many candidates think that once the interview is over, the ball is entirely in the employer's court. In reality, following up appropriately can demonstrate your professionalism, reinforce your interest, and even tip the scales in your favor when the employer is making a decision. In this chapter, we'll discuss the best strategies for post-interview communication, managing job offers, negotiating salary and benefits, and ultimately making the right career decision.

5.1 The Importance of Following Up After an Interview

Why is following up so important? Not only does it show respect for the interviewer's time, but it also keeps you top of mind as they make their decision. Employers often interview multiple candidates over several days or weeks, and a well-timed follow-up can remind them why you're the best fit for the job.

5.1.1 Reiterating Your Interest

A follow-up email allows you to reinforce your enthusiasm for the role and the company. Employers want to hire people who are genuinely excited about working with them, and a thoughtful follow-up can help convey that excitement.

5.1.2 Showcasing Your Professionalism

Employers appreciate candidates who demonstrate strong communication skills, attention to detail, and professionalism. A well-written follow-up email is a simple but effective way to show these traits.

5.1.3 Offering Additional Information

If you forgot to mention something important during the interview or thought of a question later, the follow-up email is an opportunity to provide that information or seek clarification. Just make sure your email remains concise and focused.

5.2 How and When to Send a Thank-You Email

Timing and content are key when it comes to sending a thank-you note. You want to send your email promptly, but you also need to ensure that it's polished and professional.

5.2.1 When to Send Your Thank-You Email

Ideally, you should send your thank-you email within 24 hours of the interview. This ensures that your conversation is still fresh in the interviewer's mind, while also demonstrating your promptness and enthusiasm.

5.2.2 What to Include in Your Thank-You Email

A thank-you email doesn't need to be long, but it should hit several key points. Here's what to include:
- Gratitude: Thank the interviewer for their time and consideration.
- Specific Details: Mention something specific from the interview that stood out to you, such as a particular topic you discussed, a project you're excited about, or something unique about the company.
- Reaffirm Your Interest: Reiterate why you're excited about the role and how you believe you can contribute to the company.
- Additional Information (if necessary): If relevant, provide any additional information that you didn't get to cover during the interview or offer to clarify any points.

Example Thank-You Email:

Subject Line: Thank You – [Your Name], Interview for [Position]

Email Body: "Dear [Interviewer's Name],

Thank you for taking the time to meet with me yesterday to discuss the [Position] at [Company Name]. I enjoyed our conversation about [specific detail from the interview], and it further confirmed my excitement about the opportunity to contribute to your team.

I am particularly enthusiastic about the [specific project or initiative discussed] and am confident that my experience in [relevant skill or area] will allow me to add value to your organization. Please let me know if you need any further information from me, and I look forward to hearing from you soon.

Thank you again for your time and

consideration.

Best regards,
[Your Name]"

5.2.3 Handwritten Notes vs. Email

In most cases, email is the preferred method of communication for thank-you notes due to its speed and convenience. However, for particularly formal or high-level positions, you might consider sending a handwritten note in addition to an email. Just be sure that the note is sent promptly and that your handwriting is neat and professional.

5.3 Following Up on the Status of Your Application

If you haven't heard back after the interview, it's appropriate to follow up on the status of your application. The key here is to be polite and respectful of the employer's timeline while reiterating your interest in the position.

5.3.1 When to Follow Up

Generally, it's a good idea to wait about one to two weeks after your interview before following up. This gives the employer time to review all candidates and make their decision. If the interviewer gave you a specific timeline for when they'd make a decision, wait until after that date has passed to follow up.

5.3.2 How to Follow Up

Your follow-up email should be brief and to the point. Express your continued interest in the position and politely inquire about the status of your application.

Example Follow-Up Email:

Subject Line: Follow-Up on [Position] Interview

Email Body: "Dear [Interviewer's Name],

I hope you're doing well. I wanted to follow up on the status of my application for the [Position] role. I remain very interested in the opportunity and would appreciate any updates on the next steps in the hiring process. Thank you for considering my application, and I look forward to hearing from you soon.

Best regards,
[Your Name]"

5.3.3 What to Do If You Don't Hear Back

If you still haven't heard back after sending your follow-up email, it's best to move forward with your job search. While it's disappointing, some companies take longer than others to make decisions, or they may have filled the position without notifying all candidates. In any case, staying professional and not pushing for further responses ensures you maintain a positive reputation.

5.4 Handling Job Offers

Receiving a job offer is exciting, but it's important to evaluate the offer carefully before accepting. In this section, we'll explore how to review a job offer, assess its components, and handle multiple offers.

5.4.1 Reviewing the Job Offer

When you receive an offer, take the time to review all aspects of the offer beyond just the salary. Important components include:
- Salary: Does the salary align with your expectations and industry standards?
- Benefits: Consider health insurance, retirement plans, paid time off, and any other perks like wellness programs, flexible work arrangements, or professional development opportunities.
- Work Hours: Are the hours and expectations in line with your work-life balance needs? Does the position offer remote or flexible work options if that's important to you?
- Job Responsibilities: Does the job description accurately reflect the role you want, and do you feel equipped to meet the responsibilities?
- Opportunities for Growth: Are there clear paths for career development and advancement within the company?

Pro Tip: If the offer comes over the phone, express your enthusiasm but ask for the offer in writing so you can review it in detail. It's common and professional to take a few days to evaluate the offer before responding.

5.4.2 Handling Multiple Job Offers

If you're fortunate enough to receive multiple job offers, congratulations! While it's exciting, it can also be overwhelming. Here's how to handle multiple offers:
- Evaluate the Pros and Cons: Create a list of pros and cons for each offer, considering factors like salary, benefits, job satisfaction, company culture, and growth potential.
- Communicate Professionally: If you need more time to decide, politely ask for an extension to give yourself time to weigh your options.
- Be Honest: If you've received another offer, it's okay to let the companies know—just do so diplomatically. You might say, "I've received another offer and would like to make a fully informed decision. Would it be possible to have a few more days to finalize my decision?"

5.5 Negotiating Salary and Benefits

Negotiating your salary and benefits can feel intimidating, but it's a normal and expected part of the hiring process. Employers often leave room for negotiation in their initial offer, so don't be afraid to ask for what you deserve.

5.5.1 Preparing for Salary Negotiation

Before negotiating, research the average salary for the position in your industry and geographic location. Websites like Glassdoor, Payscale, and Salary.com can provide useful insights. Make sure to consider your experience level and any special skills you bring to the table.

5.5.2 How to Negotiate Salary

When negotiating salary, be confident but respectful. Here's a structure you can follow:
1. Express Gratitude: Thank the employer for the offer and express your excitement about the opportunity.
2. State Your Case: Provide a clear, data-backed reason for why you're requesting a higher salary.
3. Propose a Range: Instead of giving a single number, propose a salary range that aligns with your research and expectations.

Example: "Thank you so much for the offer. I'm excited about the opportunity to join [Company Name] and contribute to the [Team/Project]. Based on my research and the industry standards for this role, I was hoping to discuss the possibility of a salary in the range of [Proposed Range]. Given my experience in [specific area], I believe this would be a fair reflection of the value I can bring to the team."

5.5.3 Negotiating Benefits

In addition to salary, you can negotiate benefits such as vacation time, professional development opportunities, signing bonuses, and work-from-home flexibility.

- Vacation Time: If the offered vacation time doesn't meet your expectations, you can ask for more. This is often negotiable, especially if salary increases are limited.

- Professional Development: If growth opportunities are important to you, negotiate for a budget for attending conferences, taking courses, or obtaining certifications.

- Signing Bonus: If the company is unable to meet your salary request, ask if a signing bonus is an option. This can help bridge the gap between your salary expectations and their offer.

- Work-from-Home Flexibility: If remote or flexible work arrangements are important to you, and they're not part of the offer, ask if the company would be willing to accommodate a partial or full work-from-home arrangement.

Pro Tip: When negotiating, always remain professional and collaborative. Frame your requests in terms of what's fair based on your experience and the value you'll bring to the company. Avoid making ultimatums unless you're prepared to walk away from the offer.

5.6 Accepting or Declining a Job Offer

Once you've completed your negotiations and have decided on the offer that best suits you, the next step is formally accepting or declining the offer.

5.6.1 How to Accept a Job Offer

When accepting a job offer, it's important to confirm your acceptance in writing, even if you've already discussed it verbally. This ensures that both parties are clear on the terms and start date.

Example Acceptance Email:

Subject Line: Acceptance of [Position] Offer

Email Body: "Dear [Hiring Manager's Name],

Thank you so much for the opportunity to join [Company Name] as [Position]. I am thrilled to accept the offer and look forward to contributing to the [team/project]. I've reviewed the offer and am excited to start on [start date], as agreed upon.

Please let me know if there is any additional paperwork or information needed from me before my start date. I am looking forward to joining the team!

Best regards,
[Your Name]"

5.6.2 How to Decline a Job Offer

If you've decided to decline an offer, it's important to do so graciously and professionally. You never know when your paths may cross again, so it's important to leave a positive impression, even if you're turning down the role.

Example Decline Email:

Subject Line: Declining Job Offer – [Your Name]

Email Body: "Dear [Hiring Manager's Name],

Thank you very much for offering me the opportunity to join [Company Name] as [Position]. After careful consideration, I have decided to accept another offer that I feel is a better fit for my career goals at this time. This was a difficult decision, as I was very impressed with [Company Name] and the work you are doing.

I sincerely appreciate the time you took to interview me and offer me the position, and I hope our paths may cross again in the future.

Best regards,
[Your Name]"

Pro Tip: Be prompt in declining a job offer so that the employer can move forward with other candidates.

5.7 Making the Right Career Decision

When you're evaluating multiple offers or even just one offer, it's important to consider more than just salary. You want to ensure that the job aligns with your personal values, career goals, and desired lifestyle. Here are a few factors to consider:

5.7.1 Culture and Work-Life Balance

The culture of a company plays a significant role in your overall job satisfaction. Think about whether the company's values align with yours, whether you'd enjoy working with the team, and whether the company offers a healthy work-life balance.

5.7.2 Long-Term Growth Potential

Consider where this role fits into your long-term career plans. Will the position give you opportunities to learn and grow? Is there room for advancement within the company? Does the company invest in its employees' professional development?

5.7.3 Job Stability and Security

It's important to assess the stability of the company, especially if you're joining a startup or a company in a volatile industry. Do your research on the company's financial health and growth potential to ensure that the role will offer you long-term security.

5.7.4 Location and Commute

If the position requires you to relocate or has a long commute, think about how that will impact your lifestyle. Consider whether you're comfortable with the location, housing costs, and the time you'll spend commuting.

5.7.5 Compensation and Benefits Package

While salary is important, remember to take the full benefits package into account. Health insurance, retirement plans, bonuses, and paid time off can all add significant value to your overall compensation.

> *Pro Tip: Trust your instincts. If something doesn't feel right about an offer, take the time to reevaluate whether the role is truly the right fit for you.*

Conclusion

The post-interview process is just as important as the interview itself. By following up promptly and professionally, negotiating with confidence, and carefully evaluating job offers, you can set yourself up for long-term success in your career. Remember, this phase is not just about landing any job—it's about finding the right job that aligns with your goals, values, and lifestyle. Whether you're accepting an offer or continuing your search, staying organized, informed, and proactive will ensure you make the best decisions for your future.

Chapter 6: Negotiating a Job Offer: Maximizing Your Compensation and Benefits

Negotiating a job offer can feel intimidating, but it's one of the most important steps in securing a position that not only meets your professional aspirations but also rewards you fairly for your skills and experience. In this chapter, we'll guide you through the process of negotiating salary, benefits, and other aspects of a job offer. Whether you're dealing with your first offer or considering how to approach negotiation after years in the workforce, these strategies will help you maximize your compensation package while maintaining a professional relationship with your future employer.

6.1 Why You Should Negotiate

Many job seekers are hesitant to negotiate, fearing that it may make them seem greedy or ungrateful. However, most employers expect some negotiation, and failing to advocate for yourself could result in leaving significant value on the table.

6.1.1 The Benefits of Negotiating

Improved Compensation: Negotiating your salary can have a long-term impact on your financial well-being, as future raises and bonuses are often calculated based on your starting salary.

Enhanced Benefits: Beyond salary, negotiating additional benefits such as health insurance, retirement contributions, or paid time off can increase the overall value of your compensation package.

Increased Job Satisfaction: Employees who negotiate their offers tend to feel more valued and confident in their roles, leading to higher job satisfaction.

Establishing Respect: Negotiation demonstrates that you understand your worth and are confident in your abilities, which can lead to increased respect from your employer.

6.1.2 Overcoming the Fear of Negotiation

It's normal to feel nervous about negotiating, especially if you're early in your career or if the job market is competitive. However, remember that:
- Employers Expect It: Most employers expect candidates to negotiate, so it won't come as a surprise.
- It's Professional: Approached with tact and professionalism, negotiation can enhance your image as a thoughtful and confident candidate.
- It's Your Right: You have the right to ensure that your compensation aligns with your skills, experience, and the market rate.

Pro Tip: Think of negotiation as a conversation, not a confrontation. The goal is to find a mutually beneficial solution that meets both your needs and those of the employer.

6.2 Preparing for Salary Negotiation

Preparation is crucial when negotiating salary and benefits. The more informed and confident you are, the better positioned you'll be to secure a favorable outcome.

6.2.1 Research the Market

Before entering into negotiations, it's essential to understand the typical salary range for your role, industry, and geographic location. This information will serve as a benchmark to help you gauge whether the offer is fair and where you should start your negotiation.

Key Resources for Salary Research:
- Glassdoor: Offers salary insights for specific companies, roles, and industries.
- Payscale: Provides personalized salary reports based on your job title, location, and experience level.
- Salary.com: Offers detailed salary data for different job titles and industries across various regions.
- LinkedIn Salary Insights: Uses LinkedIn data to offer salary ranges based on the job title and location.
- Company-Specific Information: If you have connections within the company or industry, ask them about the typical compensation packages for similar roles.

Pro Tip: Make sure your research accounts for geographic differences. Salaries can vary significantly based on location, cost of living, and local job market demand.

6.2.2 Assess Your Value

In addition to researching the market, assess your own unique value. What skills, experiences, and qualifications do you bring that set you apart from other candidates? Reflect on:
- Years of Experience: How many years of experience do you have in the field? Are you bringing senior-level expertise, or are you early in your career?
- Specialized Skills: Do you have any specialized skills or certifications that make you uniquely qualified for the role?
- Achievements: Have you led projects, increased sales, improved processes, or otherwise contributed to the success of your previous employers?

By understanding the value you bring, you'll feel more confident in advocating for higher compensation.

6.2.3 Decide on Your Salary Range

Before the negotiation begins, decide on the salary range you'll be comfortable with. This range should be based on your research and self-assessment.
- Your Ideal Salary: This is the highest number in your range—the salary you would love to receive, but that's still reasonable based on your research.
- Your Target Salary: This is the middle number—the amount that you believe is fair based on your experience and the market rate.
- Your Minimum Salary: This is the lowest number you're willing to accept. If an offer comes in below this number, you may need to reconsider the opportunity.

Pro Tip: Avoid providing a single number when negotiating; instead, offer a salary range to give yourself flexibility while still advocating for your desired compensation.

6.3 The Negotiation Conversation

Now that you're prepared, it's time to enter the negotiation. Whether you're negotiating salary, benefits, or both, the key is to remain calm, professional, and open to compromise.

6.3.1 When to Bring Up Salary Negotiation

The ideal time to negotiate salary is after you've received a formal offer, but before you've accepted the position. Once you've accepted the offer, your leverage to negotiate decreases significantly.

If the employer brings up salary expectations early in the interview process, you can respond by saying you'd like to learn more about the role and responsibilities before discussing compensation. This allows you to gather more information before naming a number.

6.3.2 How to Negotiate Salary

When the time comes to negotiate, follow these steps:
1. Express Enthusiasm: Start by expressing gratitude for the offer and excitement about the role. This shows that you're interested in the position and sets a positive tone for the conversation.
2. State Your Case: Present your case for a higher salary by referencing your research and the value you bring to the company. Use specific examples of your skills, experience, and achievements to demonstrate why you deserve a higher offer.
3. Propose a Range: Instead of giving a single number, propose a salary range. This allows room for negotiation while still advocating for the higher end of the range. Example: "Thank you so much for the offer. I'm excited about the opportunity to join [Company Name] as [Position]. Based on my experience in [relevant skill/industry], and considering the typical salary for this role in the market, I was

hoping we could discuss a salary in the range of [proposed range]. I believe this would be a fair reflection of the value I can bring to the team."
4. Be Ready for Counteroffers: The employer may counter with a number lower than your proposed range. Be prepared to respond by emphasizing your key strengths and considering whether the counteroffer meets your minimum salary.

6.3.3 How to Negotiate Benefits

If the employer is unable to meet your salary request, you can negotiate for additional benefits to enhance your compensation package. Some benefits to consider negotiating include:
- Vacation Time: Ask for additional paid vacation days or flexible leave policies.
- Remote Work or Flexible Hours: Negotiate for the option to work from home part-time or full-time, or to have flexible working hours.
- Signing Bonus: Request a signing bonus if the salary offer is below your expectations.
- Professional Development: Ask for funding for certifications, courses, or conferences that will help you grow in your role.
- Retirement Contributions: If the company offers a retirement plan, you may be able to negotiate higher matching contributions.

Pro Tip: Frame your requests as win-win propositions. For example, if you're asking for more vacation time, you might say, "I've found that taking time off allows me to return to work more focused and productive."

6.3.4 Responding to Common Employer Reactions

Employers may respond in a variety of ways to your negotiation. Here's how to handle some common scenarios:
- They Agree to Your Request: If the employer agrees to your salary or benefits request, express gratitude and confirm the details in writing.
- They Make a Counteroffer: If the employer counters with a lower offer, assess whether the number meets your needs. You can either accept the counteroffer, propose a compromise, or ask for additional benefits to make up the difference.
- They Can't Meet Your Request: If the employer is firm on salary but you're still interested in the role, try negotiating for other benefits, such as flexible work arrangements or professional development opportunities. If they can't offer any additional benefits, you'll need to decide whether the role is still worth accepting.

6.4 Negotiating in Special Circumstances

Certain situations call for a slightly different approach to negotiation. Here are a few scenarios you may encounter and how to handle them.

6.4.1 Negotiating as a Recent Graduate or Early-Career Professional

If you're early in your career or fresh out of college, you may feel that you have less leverage in negotiations. However, you can still negotiate, especially if you have relevant skills, internships, or certifications.

How to Approach It:

- Highlight any internships, volunteer work, or part-time jobs that gave you relevant experience.
- Emphasize your enthusiasm for learning and growing in the role.
- Be open to negotiating for non-salary benefits, such as professional development or mentorship opportunities.

6.4.2 Negotiating During an Economic Downturn

In an economic downturn, companies may have tighter budgets, and negotiating salary can be more challenging. However, this doesn't mean you should accept the first offer without question. There are ways to approach the conversation tactfully.

How to Approach It:
- Acknowledge the Economic Context: Be sensitive to the economic realities and recognize that the company may have budget constraints.
- Focus on Long-Term Value: Emphasize the value you can bring to the company and how your skills can help them navigate challenges and grow.
- Negotiate for Future Compensation: If salary increases are difficult right now, you might negotiate for a performance review after six months, with the possibility of a raise once the economic situation improves.
- Explore Alternative Benefits: If a salary increase isn't possible, focus on benefits like additional paid time off, remote work options, or signing bonuses.

6.4.3 Negotiating a Promotion or Raise

Negotiating a raise or promotion is different from negotiating an initial job offer, as you're already working for the company and likely have a track record of achievements.

How to Approach It:
- Prepare Evidence of Your Contributions: Before requesting a raise or promotion, gather data on your accomplishments, including projects you've led, revenue increases, cost savings, or other tangible impacts you've had on the company.
- Research Salary Benchmarks: Just as you would for a job offer, research what people in similar roles are earning. Use this information to make your case for a raise.
- Frame It Around Your Value: Focus the conversation on the value you've brought to the company and why you deserve additional compensation or responsibilities.

Example: "Over the past year, I've taken on additional responsibilities and contributed to increasing team productivity by 20%. Given the scope of my role and the value I bring to the team, I would like to discuss the possibility of a salary adjustment to reflect these contributions."

6.5 Finalizing the Negotiation

Once you've reached an agreement with the employer, it's essential to finalize the details in writing. This ensures that both you and the employer are on the same page regarding salary, benefits, and other terms of your employment.

6.5.1 Confirming the Offer in Writing

After the negotiation, ask for a revised offer letter or employment contract that outlines all of the terms you've agreed upon, including salary, benefits, start date, and any other negotiated details.

What to Include in the Offer Confirmation:
- Salary: Ensure the final agreed-upon salary is included, along with details about any bonuses or commission structures.
- Benefits: Confirm the details of health insurance, retirement plans, paid time off, and any other benefits you've negotiated.
- Start Date: Make sure the start date and any probationary periods are clearly stated.
- Additional Agreements: If you negotiated for things like a signing bonus, relocation assistance, or a future salary review, ensure these details are included as well.

6.5.2 Expressing Gratitude

Regardless of the outcome of the negotiation, it's important to express gratitude for the opportunity and the employer's willingness to negotiate. A positive attitude will leave a lasting impression and help start your new role on the right foot.

Example: "Thank you again for working with me to finalize the details of this offer. I'm excited about joining [Company Name] and look forward to contributing to the [team/project]. I appreciate your flexibility and consideration during this process."

6.6 Knowing When to Walk Away

While negotiating is an important part of the process, there are times when the offer simply doesn't align with your needs or expectations, and walking away is the best decision. Knowing when and how to respectfully decline an offer is key to maintaining your professionalism and reputation.

6.6.1 Signs It's Time to Walk Away

The Offer Doesn't Meet Your Minimum Requirements: If the salary or benefits fall below your minimum threshold and the employer is unable or unwilling to negotiate, it may not be the right opportunity for you.

The Company Culture or Role Isn't a Good Fit: If the interview process has revealed red flags about the company culture, work-life balance, or role responsibilities, trust your instincts and consider whether this job will truly make you happy in the long run.

You Have a Better Offer Elsewhere: If another company has made you a better offer in terms of compensation, career growth, or job satisfaction, it may be in your best interest to pursue that opportunity instead.

6.6.2 How to Decline an Offer Respectfully

If you've decided to walk away from an offer after negotiation, it's important to do so graciously. You never know when you might cross paths with the employer again, so maintaining professionalism is essential.

Example Decline Email:

Subject Line: Declining Job Offer – [Your Name]

Email Body: "Dear [Hiring Manager's

Name],

Thank you for offering me the opportunity to join [Company Name] as [Position]. After careful consideration, I have decided to pursue another opportunity that I believe is a better fit for my career goals at this time. It was a difficult decision, as I was very impressed with your team and the work [Company Name] is doing.

I greatly appreciate your time and consideration, and I hope that we may have the opportunity to work together in the future.

Best regards,
[Your Name]"

Pro Tip: Keep the email polite and brief.

You don't need to provide extensive details about why you're declining the offer unless you feel it would be helpful or necessary.

Conclusion

Negotiating a job offer is a critical step in securing compensation and benefits that reflect your worth and align with your career goals. Whether you're negotiating salary, benefits, or perks like flexible working hours, the key is to be informed, confident, and professional. Remember, negotiation is a normal part of the hiring process, and most employers expect it. By preparing thoroughly, approaching the conversation with tact, and knowing when to accept or walk away, you'll be well-positioned to maximize your compensation package and set yourself up for success in your new role.

Chapter 7: Starting a New Job Successfully: Making a Positive First Impression and Building Long-Term Success

Starting a new job is both exciting and challenging. It's your opportunity to make a strong first impression, establish positive relationships with your colleagues, and set the foundation for long-term success. The first few weeks in a new role are critical to your integration into the company's culture and your overall job satisfaction. In this chapter, we'll discuss how to prepare for your first day, build strong working relationships, navigate the onboarding process, and set yourself up for success in your new position.

7.1 Preparing for Your First Day

Your first day at a new job is often filled with orientation, meeting new colleagues, and learning the ropes of the company's processes and systems. Being well-prepared for this day can help ease any nervousness and ensure you make a positive first impression.

7.1.1 Confirm the Details

A few days before your start date, confirm the logistics of your first day to ensure everything goes smoothly.

- Start Time: Double-check the time you're expected to arrive, especially if the company has flexible work hours.

- Location: If your role is in-person or hybrid, confirm the office location and where you should report. If it's remote, ensure you have the correct link or login information for any virtual onboarding.

- Dress Code: Ask about the company's dress code and make sure you're dressed appropriately for your first day. Even if the company has a casual dress code, it's better to err on the side of being slightly more formal on your first day.

7.1.2 Organize Your Paperwork

Before your first day, make sure you've completed any necessary paperwork that HR may have sent, such as tax forms, direct deposit information, or company agreements. This ensures that you can focus on orientation and learning the role, rather than administrative tasks.

7.1.3 Get a Good Night's Sleep

Nerves can make it difficult to sleep before your first day, but it's important to get a good night's rest. Arriving well-rested will help you stay focused and energized throughout the day.

Pro Tip: Plan your morning routine the night before, including packing any necessary materials (notebook, pen, laptop, etc.) and setting out your clothes. This reduces stress and ensures you're prepared.

7.2 Making a Positive First Impression

The first impression you make on your colleagues and managers will shape how they perceive you in the future. Being polite, professional, and proactive during your first days sets the tone for your work relationships and helps you gain credibility quickly.

7.2.1 Be Punctual

Arrive on time, or even a few minutes early, on your first day. This demonstrates reliability and respect for the company's schedule. If you're working remotely, log in to virtual meetings a few minutes before they start.

7.2.2 Be Polite and Professional

Your interactions with colleagues, from the receptionist to your direct supervisor, should be courteous and professional. Greet people with a smile, introduce yourself, and show enthusiasm about joining the team.

7.2.3 Show Enthusiasm

Show excitement about the role and the company. Managers and coworkers will appreciate your enthusiasm and willingness to contribute. Express genuine curiosity about how things work and be ready to learn.

Example: If a colleague is explaining a process, say something like, "That's really interesting—thank you for walking me through it. I'm looking forward to learning more."

7.2.4 Listen and Observe

While it's important to ask questions and engage, it's equally important to listen and observe. The first few days in a new role are an opportunity to absorb as much information as possible about the company's culture, processes, and unwritten rules. Pay attention to how your colleagues interact, how decisions are made, and how work gets done.

Pro Tip: Take notes during meetings and training sessions. This will help you retain important information and show that you're actively engaged.

7.3 Navigating the Onboarding Process

Most companies have an onboarding process designed to help new employees integrate into the team, understand the company's systems, and learn about their role. Successfully navigating this process is key to your long-term success.

7.3.1 Understand the Onboarding Timeline

Find out how long the onboarding process is expected to take. Some companies have structured onboarding programs that last several weeks, while others may expect you to hit the ground running. Knowing the timeline helps you manage your expectations and gives you a sense of when you should feel fully up to speed.

7.3.2 Ask for Clarification

Don't be afraid to ask for clarification if something isn't clear. Onboarding can involve a lot of information being thrown at you in a short amount of time, and it's better to ask questions early on than to make mistakes later because you didn't understand something.

7.3.3 Learn the Company's Systems and Tools

During onboarding, you'll likely be introduced to the company's systems, such as project management tools, communication platforms (e.g., Slack or Microsoft Teams), and databases. Take the time to familiarize yourself with these tools, as they're crucial to how work gets done within the company.

> *Pro Tip: If the company uses a tool you're not familiar with, seek out tutorials or ask a colleague for guidance. This shows initiative and a willingness to learn.*

7.3.4 Meet with Key Stakeholders

During the onboarding process, you'll be introduced to various team members and departments. Make an effort to build relationships with these individuals, as they will likely be key collaborators in your work.

How to Approach It:
- Introduce Yourself: When meeting colleagues for the first time, introduce
- yourself and mention your role. Express enthusiasm about working together.
- Schedule 1:1s: If appropriate, schedule one-on-one meetings with key team members or managers to learn more about their roles and how you can collaborate effectively.
- Take Notes: As you meet people, take note of their responsibilities and how they might interact with your work. This will help you understand how the team operates and who to go to for specific questions or issues.

7.4 Building Strong Relationships with Your Team

Building strong relationships with your coworkers is essential to creating a positive work environment and setting yourself up for long-term success. Collaboration, communication, and mutual respect are the foundations of a healthy workplace dynamic.

7.4.1 Be Open and Approachable

Your first few weeks on the job are a time for you to build rapport with your colleagues. Be open and approachable by engaging in small talk, participating in team discussions, and showing interest in your coworkers' work and perspectives.

7.4.2 Offer Help

Even if you're still learning the ropes, offering to help your teammates demonstrates a collaborative mindset. Whether it's offering to assist with a project or helping someone with a task, being helpful builds goodwill and strengthens your relationships.

Example: "If there's anything I can do to help with this project, please let me know. I'd be happy to assist!"

7.4.3 Respect Team Dynamics

Every team has its own dynamics and working style. Some teams communicate frequently and collaborate closely, while others may be more independent. Take time to observe how your team functions and adapt your approach accordingly.

- If the team is collaborative: Join in on brainstorming sessions, ask for feedback, and contribute ideas.

- If the team is more independent: Focus on completing your tasks independently while maintaining open lines of communication when necessary.

Pro Tip: If you're unsure about the team's dynamics, ask your manager how best to fit in and contribute.

7.4.4 Communicate Effectively

Effective communication is key to building trust and maintaining strong working relationships. Make an effort to communicate clearly and regularly with your team, whether it's providing updates on your work, asking for feedback, or sharing insights.

- Be Responsive: Respond to emails and messages in a timely manner to show that you're engaged and reliable.

- Be Transparent: If you're facing challenges or need help, communicate that to your manager or team members. Transparency fosters trust and ensures that problems can be addressed early.

7.5 Setting Goals for Your First 90 Days

The first 90 days of a new job are critical for establishing yourself in your role and setting the foundation for your long-term success. During this time, it's important to set clear goals that will help you stay focused and measure your progress.

7.5.1 Understand Your Manager's Expectations

Early on, schedule a one-on-one meeting with your manager to discuss their expectations for your first 90 days. Understanding their priorities will help you align your efforts with what matters most to the team and the company.

Key Questions to Ask:

"What are the most important things I should focus on in my first 90 days?"

"How will my success be measured in this role?"

"What are the biggest challenges the team is currently facing, and how can I help address them?"

7.5.2 Set Short-Term and Long-Term Goals

Once you understand your manager's expectations, set specific, measurable goals for yourself. These goals should be realistic for your first 90 days but also challenge you to make meaningful contributions.

Example Short-Term Goals:

Complete onboarding and training on the company's systems within the first two weeks.

Build relationships with key stakeholders by scheduling introductory meetings with at least five team members.

Example Long-Term Goals:

Take ownership of a specific project or task by the end of the first month.

Contribute a process improvement or new idea within your first 90 days that benefits the team or department.

7.5.3 Create a 30-60-90 Day Plan

To help guide your first three months, consider creating a 30-60-90 day plan that outlines your goals and priorities at each stage.

First 30 Days: Focus on learning. Get familiar with the company's systems, processes, and culture. Build relationships with your team and understand your role.

Days 31-60: Start contributing to projects. Apply what you've learned and begin taking ownership of tasks. Continue building relationships and seek feedback from your manager and colleagues.

Days 61-90: By this time, you should be functioning independently in your role. Start looking for ways to add value by streamlining processes, proposing new ideas, or leading a small project.

> *Pro Tip: Share your 30-60-90 day plan with your manager for feedback. This demonstrates your initiative and ensures that your goals are aligned with the team's priorities.*

7.6 Seeking Feedback and Continuous Improvement

Regular feedback is essential to your growth in a new role. By seeking feedback early and often, you can adjust your approach, improve your performance, and demonstrate your commitment to self-development.

7.6.1 Ask for Feedback Regularly

Don't wait for formal performance reviews to ask for feedback. After completing a project or task, ask your manager or colleagues for input on how you can improve.

Example: "I'd appreciate your feedback on the project I completed last week. Are there any areas where I can improve or do things differently next time?"

7.6.2 Be Open to Constructive Criticism

Receiving feedback—especially constructive criticism—can be challenging, but it's an invaluable tool for your professional growth. Approach feedback with an open mind and a willingness to learn.

How to Handle Constructive Criticism:
- Listen Actively: Pay attention to the feedback without interrupting or getting defensive.
- Ask Questions: If something isn't clear, ask for clarification so you can understand how to improve.

- Take Action: Use the feedback to make changes to your approach or performance. This shows that you're serious about self-improvement.

7.6.3 Track Your Progress

Keep track of the feedback you receive and the progress you make in response to it. This can be useful for future performance reviews and helps you see how much you've grown since starting the job.

Pro Tip: Consider keeping a journal of your accomplishments, challenges, and areas for improvement. This will help you reflect on your development and prepare for future discussions with your manager.

7.7 Managing Work-Life Balance in a New Role

Starting a new job can be demanding, and it's easy to get caught up in the excitement of proving yourself. However, maintaining a healthy work-life balance is critical to avoiding burnout and ensuring long-term success in your role.

7.7.1 Set Boundaries Early

From the start, establish clear boundaries around your work hours and availability. If the company has a flexible work culture, clarify when you're available for meetings or collaboration.

Example: "I typically start my workday at 8 a.m. and wrap up around 5 p.m., but

I'm happy to adjust if there's an urgent need."

7.7.2 Avoid Overcommitting

In an effort to impress your new colleagues, you may be tempted to take on more work than you can handle. While it's important to show initiative, be mindful of your capacity and don't overcommit.

- Prioritize: Focus on high-impact tasks and projects that align with your role and goals.

- Communicate: If your workload becomes unmanageable, have a conversation with your manager to reprioritize tasks or seek additional support.

7.7.3 Make Time for Breaks

Regular breaks throughout the day can boost productivity and reduce stress. Whether it's a short walk, a coffee break, or stepping away from your desk for lunch, taking time to recharge is essential.

7.8 Dealing with Challenges in a New Role

Starting a new job is rarely without its challenges, and it's normal to experience some bumps along the way. How you handle these challenges can significantly impact your success and job satisfaction.

7.8.1 Navigating Unclear Expectations

Sometimes the responsibilities or expectations of your role may not be clearly defined, especially if you're joining a startup or a rapidly changing organization.

- Seek Clarity: If you're unsure about your responsibilities, ask your manager for clarification on priorities and expectations. It's better to address confusion early than to make mistakes down the road.

- Be Proactive: If you notice gaps or areas where processes could be improved, take the initiative to address them. Your proactive approach can help shape your role and add value to the company.

7.8.2 Handling Miscommunications

Miscommunications are common in any workplace, especially when you're still learning the company's culture and communication style. If a miscommunication occurs, handle it professionally.

- Clarify: Politely clarify the issue with the person involved to ensure everyone is on the same page moving forward.

- Own Your Mistakes: If the miscommunication was your fault, take responsibility and outline how you'll avoid similar issues in the future.

7.8.3 Overcoming Imposter Syndrome

Imposter syndrome — the feeling that you're not qualified or capable enough for your role — can affect even the most accomplished professionals. If you experience self-doubt, remember that you were hired for a reason and that it's normal to feel uncertain in a new role.

- Focus on Growth: Remind yourself that you're still learning and that mistakes are part of the process.

- Seek Support: Talk to a mentor or trusted colleague about your feelings. They can offer perspective and reassurance that you're on the right track.

Conclusion

Starting a new job is both exciting and challenging, but by preparing thoroughly, building strong relationships, and setting clear goals, you can set yourself up for long-term success. The first few months are an opportunity to make a lasting positive impression, understand the company's culture, and demonstrate your value. By seeking feedback, maintaining a healthy work-life balance, and addressing challenges with professionalism, you'll quickly establish yourself as a key contributor and set the foundation for a fulfilling and successful career.

Chapter 8: Setting Yourself Up for Long-Term Career Growth: Advancing in Your Role and Developing Key Skills

After you've settled into your new role, the next important step is focusing on long-term career growth. It's not enough to just perform well in your job—you need to actively plan and work toward advancing your career.

Whether you want to climb the corporate ladder, become an expert in your field, or transition into a new industry, setting clear goals and continuously developing your skills is essential for sustained success. This chapter will cover how to create a career growth plan, develop key skills, seek out opportunities for advancement, and build a network that supports your professional journey.

8.1 Defining Your Career Goals

Career growth doesn't happen by accident—it requires a clear understanding of what you want to achieve and a plan to get there. The first step is to define your long-term career goals and break them down into actionable steps.

8.1.1 Setting SMART Career Goals

A good starting point for defining your career goals is using the SMART framework: Specific, Measurable, Achievable, Relevant, and Time-bound.

- Specific: Your goal should be clear and specific. Avoid vague goals like "I want to be successful" and instead focus on concrete objectives like "I want to become a senior manager within my department."

- Measurable: Make sure you can measure your progress. For example, instead of "I want to be a better leader,"

- you could aim to lead a successful project that improves team productivity by 20%.

- Achievable: Set goals that are realistic given your current skills, experience, and resources. While it's good to aim high, setting unattainable goals can lead to frustration.

- Relevant: Your goals should align with your broader career aspirations. For example, if you want to become a marketing director, focusing on skills like data analysis and digital strategy would be relevant.

- Time-bound: Set a deadline for achieving your goals. This keeps you accountable and gives you a timeframe to work within.

Example of a SMART Goal:
"I want to earn a project management certification (Specific) within the next 12 months (Time-bound) to improve my leadership skills (Relevant) and manage three company projects with successful outcomes by the end of next year (Measurable and Achievable)."

8.1.2 Identifying Short-Term and Long-Term Goals

It's helpful to distinguish between short-term and long-term goals. Short-term goals focus on immediate steps you can take to grow in your current role, while long-term goals involve where you see yourself in five or ten years.

Short-Term Goals: These can include improving a specific skill, taking on a new project, or networking with key stakeholders within your organization. These goals are typically achievable within six months to a year.

Long-Term Goals: These focus on bigger career aspirations, such as moving into a leadership role, starting your own business, or transitioning into a new industry. Long-term goals typically take three to five years (or longer) to achieve.

> *Pro Tip: Revisit and revise your goals regularly. As your career evolves, your goals may shift, so it's important to remain flexible and update them as necessary.*

8.2 Developing Key Skills for Career Growth

Continual skill development is the cornerstone of long-term career growth. No matter what industry you're in, new trends, technologies, and best practices are constantly emerging. Staying competitive means continuously building both your hard and soft skills.

8.2.1 Hard Skills vs. Soft Skills

Understanding the difference between hard and soft skills can help you identify areas for improvement.

- Hard Skills: These are technical skills specific to your job or industry. Examples include data analysis, coding, project management, financial modeling, or proficiency in specific software tools. Hard skills are often measurable and can be demonstrated through certifications or hands-on work.

- Soft Skills: These are interpersonal and behavioral skills that are transferable across roles and industries. Examples include communication, leadership, problem-solving, adaptability, and emotional intelligence. Soft skills are crucial for building relationships, leading teams, and navigating workplace challenges.

8.2.2 Identifying Skills You Need to Develop

Start by evaluating your current skills against the requirements of your desired role. Look at job descriptions for positions you aspire to and identify any gaps between your current skill set and the qualifications needed.

How to Identify Skills to Develop:
- Review Job Descriptions: Look for common skills required for the roles you want to pursue in the future.
- Ask for Feedback: Seek feedback from your manager or mentor about areas where you can improve.
- Self-Assessment: Use online self-assessment tools or take time to reflect on your own strengths and weaknesses.

Pro Tip: Consider not only the technical skills needed for your role but also the industry trends. For example, if you're in marketing, developing skills in areas like data analytics, automation, or content marketing may be key to staying relevant.

8.2.3 Pursuing Professional Development

Once you've identified the skills you need to develop, take action to build them. There are numerous ways to pursue professional development, depending on your goals and the resources available to you.

Ways to Develop Skills:
- Online Courses: Websites like Coursera, LinkedIn Learning, Udemy, and edX offer a wide range of courses in various fields.
- Certifications: Earning industry-recognized certifications can enhance your resume and demonstrate proficiency in a specific skill set.
- Workshops and Seminars: Attend industry-specific workshops or seminars to learn from experts and network with other professionals.
- Mentorship: A mentor can provide guidance and insight on developing the skills necessary for career advancement.
- On-the-Job Learning: Take on new projects or responsibilities that challenge you to grow and learn new skills in your current role.

Pro Tip: Incorporate skill development into your daily routine. Set aside a few hours each week to focus on learning something new, whether through reading, online courses, or hands-on practice.

8.3 Seeking Opportunities for Advancement

Opportunities for advancement won't always fall into your lap—you need to actively seek them out. This could involve taking on new responsibilities, volunteering for challenging projects, or positioning yourself as a leader within your team.

8.3.1 Take Initiative and Be Proactive

One of the best ways to advance in your career is to consistently go above and beyond in your current role. Look for ways to add value by solving problems, improving processes, or taking ownership of key projects.

Ways to Take Initiative:
- Volunteer for Challenging Projects: Show that you're willing to take on tough assignments. These projects often lead to more visibility and recognition from leadership.
- Propose New Ideas: If you see opportunities for process improvements, cost savings, or new strategies, propose them to your manager or team. Being proactive in identifying solutions can make you stand out as a valuable team member.
- Mentor Others: Offering to mentor junior colleagues or help onboard new employees demonstrates leadership skills and a commitment to the success of the team.

8.3.2 Network Within Your Organization

Building relationships within your organization can open doors to advancement opportunities. Networking internally helps you stay informed about new roles, company initiatives, or upcoming projects that could help you grow.

Ways to Network Internally:
- Attend Company Events: Participate in company-wide meetings, training sessions, or social events to get to know colleagues outside your immediate team.
- Cross-Department Collaboration: Seek opportunities to work on cross-functional projects with colleagues from other departments. This can broaden your skill set and expose you to different areas of the business.
- Stay Visible to Leadership: Keep leadership informed of your contributions by sharing updates on your progress and results in team meetings or reports.

Pro Tip: Don't be afraid to advocate for yourself. If you're interested in a promotion or a specific project, let your manager know. They may not be aware of your ambitions unless you communicate them.

8.3.3 Find a Mentor or Sponsor

A mentor can provide valuable advice and guidance as you navigate your career path, while a sponsor is someone within the organization who advocates for you when opportunities for promotion arise.

How to Find a Mentor:
- Identify Potential Mentors: Look for someone within your company or industry who has experience in the areas where you want to grow.
- Reach Out: Send a polite, professional message expressing your admiration for their work and asking if they'd be open to meeting for coffee or a brief conversation.
- Build a Relationship: Be respectful of their time and seek to build a long-term relationship by showing genuine interest in their advice and applying it to your career.

8.4 Building a Strong Professional Network

Your network is one of the most powerful tools for career advancement. A strong professional network can provide you with job leads, mentorship, and opportunities for collaboration.

8.4.1 Networking Strategies

Effective networking is about building meaningful, long-term relationships, not just collecting business cards. Whether you're attending industry events, joining professional organizations, or connecting on LinkedIn, focus on creating genuine connections with people.

Networking Tips:
- Be Genuine: Show interest in others' work and career journeys. Ask thoughtful questions and listen actively.
- Provide Value: Networking is a two-way street. Offer to help others with introductions, advice, or sharing your own expertise.
- Follow Up: After meeting someone new, follow up with a message thanking them for their time and expressing interest in staying in touch.

8.4.2 Leveraging LinkedIn for Career Growth

LinkedIn is one of the most powerful tools for building and maintaining a professional network. It allows you to connect with colleagues, industry leaders, and potential employers while showcasing your expertise.

How to Leverage LinkedIn for Career Growth:
- Optimize Your Profile: Make sure your LinkedIn profile is up to date with a professional photo, a compelling headline, and a well-written summary that

highlights your skills, achievements, and career goals. Include measurable accomplishments and keywords relevant to your industry.
- Engage Regularly: Don't just passively use LinkedIn — engage with content regularly. Like, comment on, and share posts from your network. Write your own posts to share insights, industry trends, or professional updates.
- Join LinkedIn Groups: Participate in LinkedIn groups related to your field or industry. Engaging in group discussions can help you meet new people, share knowledge, and stay informed about the latest trends.
- Network with Intention: Use LinkedIn to connect with colleagues, mentors, industry leaders, and people whose careers you admire. Send personalized connection requests rather than using the default message, explaining why you'd like to connect.

Example Connection Message: "Hi [Name], I've been following your work in [Industry] and am impressed with your expertise. I'd love to connect and learn more about your approach to [specific area]. Looking forward to staying in touch!"

Pro Tip: Regularly update your profile with new projects, certifications, or skills. This ensures your profile reflects your latest accomplishments and keeps you visible to recruiters and industry professionals.

8.5 Embracing Continuous Learning and Adaptability

In today's fast-changing world, continuous learning and adaptability are crucial for long-term career growth. The skills that got you your current role may not be the same skills you'll need for your next one. By committing to lifelong learning, you can stay ahead of industry trends and remain competitive in the job market.

8.5.1 Stay Informed About Industry Trends

No matter your industry, staying up to date on the latest trends and developments is essential. Make a habit of reading industry news, following thought leaders, and attending relevant conferences or webinars.

Ways to Stay Informed:
- Read Industry Blogs and Publications: Subscribe to newsletters, blogs, and publications that are relevant to your field.
- Follow Thought Leaders: Identify key figures in your industry and follow them on LinkedIn, Twitter, or other social media platforms.
- Attend Conferences and Webinars: Participate in industry conferences, seminars, or webinars to learn from experts and expand your network.

8.5.2 Adapt to New Technologies

Technology is rapidly changing the landscape of many industries. Staying on top of emerging tools, platforms, and trends will help you remain competitive and open to new opportunities.

Examples of Adapting to New Technologies:
- Digital Marketing: Staying current on trends like AI in marketing, automation tools, and social media algorithms can help you advance in digital marketing roles.
- Software Development: Continually learning new programming languages or frameworks is essential for developers to stay competitive in their field.
- Healthcare: Adapting to new medical technologies, electronic health records (EHR), or telehealth platforms is crucial for healthcare professionals.

8.5.3 Commit to Lifelong Learning

Lifelong learning is a mindset that embraces continuous improvement, both professionally and personally. The more you invest in your education, the more value you can bring to your role and career.

Ways to Embrace Lifelong Learning:
- Take Online Courses: Continuously take online courses to learn new skills or gain deeper expertise in your field.
- Seek Feedback: Regularly ask for feedback from peers, mentors, and supervisors to identify areas for growth.
- Join Professional Associations: Become an active member of professional associations where you can access learning resources, certifications, and networking opportunities.

Pro Tip: Keep a learning journal where you record new skills or insights you gain throughout your career. This helps you track your progress and identify areas where you may want to focus in the future.

8.6 Building Your Personal Brand

A strong personal brand can set you apart in a competitive job market and open doors to new opportunities. Your personal brand is the image you project through your professional presence, skills, values, and reputation.

8.6.1 Define Your Brand

Start by defining what you want to be known for. Your personal brand should reflect your core skills, areas of expertise, and professional values.

Ask yourself:
- What are my strengths?
- What unique value do I bring to my industry or role?
- What do I want to be known for in my career?

8.6.2 Build an Online Presence

In today's digital world, having an online presence is essential to building your personal brand. LinkedIn is a great platform for this, but you can also use personal websites, blogs, or other social media channels to showcase your expertise.

Ways to Build an Online Presence:
- Create Content: Write articles, blog posts, or social media posts that showcase your knowledge and insights in your field.
- Share Your Work: Use platforms like LinkedIn or a personal website to share case studies, project outcomes, or examples of your work.
- Engage in Industry Conversations: Participate in online discussions or comment on relevant industry trends to position yourself as an active participant in your field.

8.6.3 Be Consistent

Consistency is key when building a personal brand. Ensure that your messaging, online profiles, and interactions align with the image you want to project.

> *Pro Tip: Think of your personal brand as an ongoing project. It's not something you create once and forget about—regularly update and refine it as your career evolves.*

Conclusion

Setting yourself up for long-term career growth requires a combination of goal-setting, continuous learning, skill development, and networking. By defining your career goals, actively seeking opportunities for advancement, and building a strong professional network, you can position yourself for success.

Chapter 9: Leadership and Team Dynamics: Leading Effectively and Contributing to a Positive Workplace Culture

As you progress in your career, leadership and team dynamics become critical components of your success. Whether you're leading a team directly or contributing to a project as part of a group, understanding how to manage relationships, communicate effectively, and inspire others is essential. Leadership is not just about having a formal title—it's about fostering collaboration, motivating others, and cultivating a positive and productive workplace culture. In this chapter, we'll cover what it takes to be an effective leader, how to manage team dynamics, and how to build and maintain a healthy workplace culture.

9.1 Understanding Leadership: Beyond Titles and Authority

Leadership is often associated with titles and positions, but true leadership goes beyond formal authority. It's about influencing, inspiring, and empowering others, regardless of your job title. Whether you're a team lead, project manager, or individual contributor, adopting a leadership mindset is essential for career advancement.

9.1.1 The Difference Between Leadership and Management

While management focuses on overseeing tasks, processes, and resources, leadership is about setting a vision, inspiring others, and building a team culture. Both skills are important, but effective leaders know how to balance managing day-to-day operations with leading people toward long-term success.

Key Differences:
- Management: Focuses on processes, tasks, and maintaining control. Managers ensure that goals are met, deadlines are adhered to, and resources are allocated efficiently.
- Leadership: Focuses on people, vision, and motivation. Leaders inspire and guide their teams, helping them grow, innovate, and work toward a common goal.

9.1.2 Leadership Styles

There are several different leadership styles, and understanding which one works best for you—and when to adapt your style—is crucial.

Some common leadership styles include:
- Transformational Leadership: Focused on inspiring and motivating team members to exceed expectations and embrace change. This style is ideal for driving innovation and fostering personal development.
- Transactional Leadership: Based on clear structures, rewards, and penalties. This style works well in environments where adherence to rules and standards is essential for success.

- Servant Leadership: Focuses on serving the team and putting the needs of others first. Servant leaders prioritize the well-being and development of their team members, creating a supportive and empowering environment.
- Democratic Leadership: Encourages team participation and collaboration in decision-making. This style helps build trust and fosters a sense of ownership among team members.
- Autocratic Leadership: Involves making decisions independently with little input from team members. While this style can be effective in high-pressure or time-sensitive situations, it may limit creativity and team buy-in.

Pro Tip: Great leaders adapt their style to the needs of their team and the specific situation. Flexibility and emotional intelligence are key to successful leadership.

9.2 Essential Leadership Skills

To be an effective leader, you need to develop a variety of skills that go beyond technical expertise. Leadership requires emotional intelligence, communication, and decision-making abilities, as well as the ability to guide and develop others.

9.2.1 Emotional Intelligence (EQ)

Emotional intelligence is the ability to understand and manage your own emotions while being aware of and empathetic to the emotions of others. Leaders with high emotional intelligence can build strong relationships, navigate conflicts, and motivate their teams more effectively.

Components of Emotional Intelligence:
- Self-awareness: Understanding your emotions, strengths, weaknesses, and w your actions impact others.
- Self-regulation: Controlling your emotions and responses in difficult situations, staying calm under pressure.
- Motivation: Being driven to achieve and setting an example of dedication and work ethic for your team.
- Empathy: Recognizing and understanding the emotions of others, and considering their feelings when making decisions.
- Social Skills: Building rapport, managing relationships, and fostering collaboration within your team.

9.2.2 Effective Communication

Leaders must be able to communicate clearly, confidently, and persuasively. Communication isn't just about conveying information—it's about ensuring that your message is understood, inspiring action, and fostering open dialogue.

Effective Communication Techniques:
- Active Listening: Pay attention to what others are saying without interrupting, and ask clarifying questions to ensure understanding.
- Transparency: Be open and honest with your team about expectations, challenges, and decisions.
- Feedback: Provide constructive feedback regularly, focusing on how team members can improve and recognizing their successes.
- Nonverbal Communication: Be aware of body language, tone of voice, and facial expressions, as they play a significant role in how your message is received.

9.2.3 Decision-Making

Leaders are often responsible for making tough decisions that impact their teams and the organization. Effective decision-making involves gathering information, considering various perspectives, and weighing the pros and cons before taking action.

Decision-Making Tips:
- Analyze the Situation: Gather all relevant data and input before making a decision.
- Consider Long-Term Impact: Think beyond the immediate outcomes and consider how your decision will affect the team and organization in the long term.
- Involve the Team: When appropriate, involve team members in the decision-making process to get diverse perspectives and build buy-in.
- Be Decisive: Once you've made a decision, communicate it clearly and confidently, and be prepared to stand by it.

9.2.4 Delegation

Effective leaders know how to delegate tasks to their team members based on their strengths and areas of expertise. Delegation empowers your team, improves efficiency, and frees you up to focus on higher-level tasks.

How to Delegate Effectively:
- Know Your Team's Strengths: Understand each team member's skills, strengths, and career goals to delegate tasks that align with their capabilities.
- Set Clear Expectations: Provide clear instructions and desired outcomes when delegating tasks, and give team members the autonomy to complete the work.
- Trust Your Team: Once you've delegated a task, trust that your team members will handle it without micromanaging.

Follow Up: Check in periodically to ensure that progress is being made and offer support if needed.

9.2.5 Conflict Resolution

Conflict is inevitable in any team environment, but strong leaders know how to address and resolve conflicts in a constructive way. Leaders who can manage conflicts effectively help maintain team cohesion and create a positive work environment.

Steps to Resolve Conflict:
- Identify the Source: Determine the root cause of the conflict and the parties involved.
- Facilitate Open Communication: Encourage the individuals involved to express their perspectives and listen to each other's concerns.
- Find Common Ground: Look for areas of agreement and work together to develop a solution that satisfies both parties.
- Focus on Solutions, Not Blame: Keep the conversation focused on resolving the issue rather than assigning blame.

9.3 Building Strong Team Dynamics

A high-performing team doesn't just happen—it's built on trust, collaboration, and clear communication. As a leader, fostering positive team dynamics is essential for achieving collective goals and maintaining a productive work environment.

9.3.1 Building Trust

Trust is the foundation of any successful team. When team members trust one another and their leader, they're more likely to take risks, share ideas, and work collaboratively.

How to Build Trust:
- Be Consistent: Consistency in your actions and words builds reliability. Follow through on your commitments and be transparent with your team.
- Encourage Open Communication: Create an environment where team members feel comfortable sharing their thoughts and concerns without fear of judgment.
- Model Integrity: Lead by example by demonstrating honesty, fairness, and ethical behavior in all interactions.

9.3.2 Encouraging Collaboration

Collaboration is key to achieving team goals. Leaders should foster an environment where team members can work together, share ideas, and support one another.

How to Foster Collaboration:
- Promote Open Dialogue: Encourage team members to share their ideas and opinions, and facilitate discussions where different perspectives are valued.
- Set Team Goals: Establish clear, shared goals that the team can work toward collectively. This helps align individual efforts and keeps everyone focused on the bigger picture.

- Provide Opportunities for Teamwork: Assign projects that require collaboration and create opportunities for team members to work together across departments or functions.

9.3.3 Recognizing and Celebrating Success

Celebrating team successes, both big and small, boosts morale and motivates team members to continue performing at a high level. Recognition is one of the most powerful tools for building a positive team culture.

Ways to Recognize Success:
- Public Recognition: Acknowledge team members' achievements during meetings or in company-wide communications.
- Personalized Appreciation: Take the time to personally thank individuals for their hard work, either in person or through a note.
- Incentives and Rewards: Offer rewards such as bonuses, time off, or other incentives for exceptional performance.

Pro Tip: Recognition should be timely, specific, and genuine. When team members know their efforts are appreciated, they're more likely to stay engaged and motivated.

9.4 Fostering a Positive Workplace Culture

A positive workplace culture is one where employees feel valued, respected, and motivated to contribute their best work. As a leader, you play a critical role in shaping and maintaining the culture of your team and the organization.

9.4.1 Lead by Example

Leaders set the tone for workplace culture through their actions, behaviors, and attitudes. By modeling the values and behaviors you want to see in your team, you create an environment where those values become ingrained in the workplace culture.

How to Lead by Example:
- Demonstrate Integrity: Uphold ethical standards in all your interactions, and be transparent and honest with your team.
- Show Respect: Treat every team member with respect, regardless of their position. Value their contributions and listen to their ideas.
- Maintain a Positive Attitude: Your attitude as a leader is contagious. Stay optimistic and solution-oriented, even in challenging situations.
- Prioritize Work-Life Balance: Encourage a healthy work-life balance by setting boundaries, respecting personal time, and leading by example. Avoid overworking yourself or expecting your team to work beyond reasonable hours.

9.4.2 Promote Inclusivity and Diversity

A diverse and inclusive workplace brings different perspectives, fosters innovation, and improves problem-solving. As a leader, you must create an environment where everyone feels included, respected, and valued for their unique contributions.

How to Promote Inclusivity:
- Encourage Diverse Perspectives: In team discussions and brainstorming sessions, actively seek input from individuals with different backgrounds, experiences, and viewpoints.
- Address Biases: Be aware of unconscious biases that may influence decision-making or team dynamics. Actively work to create an environment free from discrimination.
- Celebrate Diversity: Recognize and celebrate the diverse cultural backgrounds and experiences of your team members. This can be done through team-building activities, events, or simply acknowledging different cultural holidays and traditions.

9.4.3 Encourage Open Communication

A positive workplace culture thrives when employees feel comfortable expressing their ideas, concerns, and feedback. As a leader, it's your responsibility to create a safe space for open communication.

How to Foster Open Communication:

- Hold Regular Check-Ins: Schedule one-on-one meetings with team members to discuss their progress, challenges, and career goals. These meetings also provide an opportunity for employees to share any concerns in a private setting.
- Create Feedback Loops: Encourage ongoing feedback from your team, not just during performance reviews. Show that you value their input and are willing to make improvements based on their feedback.
- Address Conflicts Early: When issues arise, address them promptly and professionally. Avoiding conflicts can create tension and damage team morale, whereas resolving them quickly fosters trust.

9.4.4 Support Employee Development

A strong workplace culture is one that invests in the growth and development of its employees. By providing opportunities for learning, mentorship, and career advancement, you show your team that you're committed to their long-term success.

Ways to Support Employee Development:
- Offer Professional Development Opportunities: Encourage team members to attend workshops, webinars, and training sessions to enhance their skills.

- Provide Mentorship: Either act as a mentor yourself or pair team members with mentors within the organization to guide their development and provide career advice.
- Promote from Within: Whenever possible, promote internal candidates to leadership roles. This shows employees that there's room for growth within the company and that hard work is rewarded.

Pro Tip: Regularly discuss career aspirations with your team members and help them map out a development plan. Employees who feel supported in their growth are more likely to stay engaged and committed to the organization.

9.5 Leading Through Change

Change is inevitable in any organization, and how you lead through it can make or break your team's success. Whether it's a company restructuring, a shift in strategy, or the introduction of new technology, effective leaders know how to manage change while keeping their teams motivated and focused.

9.5.1 Communicate the Vision

When leading through change, it's important to clearly communicate the vision and reasons behind the change. Team members are more likely to embrace change if they understand how it aligns with the company's goals and how it benefits them.

How to Communicate Change:
- Be Transparent: Explain the rationale for the change and what the expected outcomes are. Be honest about potential challenges.
- Connect the Dots: Help team members see how the change affects them personally and how their contributions will play a role in the transition.
- Answer Questions: Be open to questions and address concerns in a timely manner. Create an open dialogue to help your team feel more comfortable with the change.

9.5.2 Provide Support During Transitions

Change can be stressful, so it's important to offer your team support throughout the process. This could involve additional training, resources, or just being available to address concerns.

Ways to Support Your Team:
- Provide Training: If new tools, systems, or processes are being introduced, ensure your team has the training and resources they need to succeed.
- Offer Flexibility: Be patient and flexible as your team adapts to the change. Some employees may need more time to adjust than others.

- Check In Regularly: During periods of change, increase the frequency of your check-ins to gauge how your team is handling the transition. Address any issues before they escalate.

9.5.3 Stay Positive and Resilient

Change can bring uncertainty, but as a leader, it's your job to stay positive and resilient. Your team will look to you for reassurance and guidance, so it's important to model a calm and optimistic attitude, even in the face of challenges.

Pro Tip: Acknowledge the difficulties of change, but also focus on the opportunities it presents. This balanced approach helps your team stay focused on the benefits of the transition rather than the challenges.

Conclusion

Being an effective leader and managing team dynamics requires a combination of emotional intelligence, communication skills, and the ability to inspire and guide others. Leadership goes beyond managing tasks — it's about building trust, fostering collaboration, and creating a positive workplace culture where people feel valued and empowered to succeed. Whether you're leading a team or contributing to one, the principles of good leadership — such as transparency, inclusivity, and adaptability — are essential for long-term career growth and organizational success. As you continue to develop your leadership skills, remember that great leaders are always learning, adapting, and growing alongside their teams.

Chapter 10: Maintaining a Healthy Work-Life Balance: Balancing Career Ambitions with Personal Well-Being

As you advance in your career, maintaining a healthy work-life balance becomes increasingly important. While professional success is a key goal for many, it's crucial to balance your career ambitions with personal well-being. A poor work-life balance can lead to stress, burnout, and decreased productivity, while a healthy balance can improve your job satisfaction, relationships, and overall quality of life. In this chapter, we'll explore strategies for managing your time effectively, setting boundaries, avoiding burnout, and ensuring that your personal and professional lives are harmonious.

10.1 Understanding Work-Life Balance

Work-life balance refers to the ability to divide your time and energy between work responsibilities and personal life in a way that promotes overall well-being. Achieving this balance doesn't mean spending equal amounts of time on both, but rather finding a balance that allows you to excel in your career while maintaining your physical, mental, and emotional health.

10.1.1 The Importance of Work-Life Balance

Maintaining a healthy balance between your professional and personal lives is essential for several reasons:
- Prevents Burnout: Consistently overworking without adequate rest and recovery can lead to burnout, which affects both your mental and physical health. A healthy balance allows for proper rest and reduces the risk of long-term exhaustion.
- Improves Job Satisfaction: When you have time to recharge and pursue activities outside of work, you're more likely to feel satisfied and energized in your job.
- Boosts Productivity: Rest and relaxation improve your focus, creativity, and problem-solving skills. A well-rested employee is far more productive than one who is constantly drained.
- Strengthens Personal Relationships: Time spent with family, friends, and loved ones helps maintain strong personal relationships, which are key to overall happiness and well-being.

10.1.2 Signs of an Imbalance

Recognizing when your work-life balance is off can help you take proactive steps to address the issue. Some signs that you may be struggling with imbalance include:
- Constant Fatigue: You feel tired all the time, even after a full night's sleep, and have trouble focusing on tasks.
- Frequent Stress: You're frequently anxious or stressed about work, and it spills over into your personal life.

- Lack of Time for Personal Life: You rarely spend time with family, friends, or on personal hobbies because work consumes the majority of your time.
- Physical and Emotional Burnout: You feel emotionally drained, physically exhausted, and disinterested in both work and personal activities.

If you notice any of these signs, it's important to reevaluate your workload and daily routines to restore balance.

10.2 Setting Boundaries

Setting clear boundaries between work and personal life is one of the most effective ways to achieve and maintain a healthy work-life balance. Boundaries help you protect your personal time, reduce stress, and prevent work from dominating your life.

10.2.1 Setting Work Hours

Whether you work in an office or remotely, it's important to establish and stick to regular work hours. Defining a clear start and end time to your workday helps you prevent work from bleeding into your personal time.

How to Set Work Hours:
- Communicate with Your Team: Let your manager and colleagues know your availability. Set expectations that you will respond to work-related communications only during certain hours.
- Stick to Your Schedule: It's easy to extend your workday, especially when working remotely, but doing so regularly can lead to burnout. Be disciplined about logging off at the end of the day.
- Use Time Management Tools: Tools like calendar apps and time-blocking techniques can help you stay organized and ensure that work tasks are completed during your designated hours.

10.2.2 Establishing Personal Boundaries

Personal boundaries are just as important as professional ones. Protecting your personal time ensures that you have space for activities outside of work that contribute to your overall well-being.

How to Establish Personal Boundaries:
- Prioritize Personal Time: Schedule personal activities like family time, exercise, and hobbies just as you would schedule meetings or work tasks. Treat this time as non-negotiable.
- Say No When Necessary: Learn to say no to extra tasks or projects that might overload your schedule, especially if they interfere with your personal time.
- Avoid Work During Off-Hours: Avoid checking work emails or messages during weekends, evenings, or vacations unless absolutely necessary.

10.2.3 Managing Remote Work Boundaries

For those working remotely, the line between personal and professional life can easily blur. It's important to set boundaries that allow you to separate work from home life.

Tips for Managing Remote Work Boundaries:
- Create a Designated Workspace: Set up a dedicated workspace that you can physically leave at the end of the day, even if it's just a corner of your living room.
- Set Clear Start and End Times: Just as in an office environment, set clear times for starting and ending your workday.
- Communicate with Family or Housemates: If you live with others, communicate your work hours and create boundaries around interruptions during work time.

10.3 Time Management Strategies

Effective time management is crucial for maintaining a healthy work-life balance. By managing your time efficiently, you can accomplish your professional tasks without letting work spill over into your personal life.

10.3.1 Prioritizing Tasks

One of the keys to effective time management is learning how to prioritize tasks. Not all tasks are equally important or urgent, so it's important to focus on what matters most.

How to Prioritize:
- Use the Eisenhower Matrix: This method categorizes tasks into four quadrants based on urgency and importance:
  - Urgent and Important: Do these tasks immediately.
  - Important but Not Urgent: Schedule these tasks for later.
  - Urgent but Not Important: Delegate these tasks if possible.
  - Not Urgent or Important: Consider eliminating or postponing these tasks.
- Focus on High-Impact Activities: Prioritize tasks that will have the biggest impact on your goals and objectives. Avoid spending too much time on low-value tasks that don't contribute significantly to your progress.

10.3.2 Time Blocking

Time blocking is a powerful technique for managing your schedule. By allocating specific blocks of time for different activities, you can improve focus and productivity while ensuring you have time for personal activities.

How to Use Time Blocking:
- Plan Your Day in Advance: At the start of the day or week, plan out your schedule by blocking out time for specific tasks and activities.

- Include Breaks and Personal Time: Be sure to block time for breaks, meals, and personal activities. This ensures that you're not working nonstop throughout the day.
- Stick to the Schedule: Follow your time blocks as closely as possible, but allow for flexibility if urgent tasks arise.

10.3.3 Avoiding Multitasking

While multitasking might seem like an efficient way to get things done, it often leads to decreased productivity and increased stress. Focus on one task at a time to improve the quality of your work and reduce mental fatigue.

Why Multitasking Is Ineffective:
- Decreases Focus: Switching between tasks can make it difficult to focus on any one thing, leading to mistakes and incomplete work.
- Increases Stress: Trying to manage multiple tasks at once can feel overwhelming and increase stress levels.
- Lowers Productivity: Studies show that multitasking actually slows you down, as your brain needs time to adjust each time you switch tasks.

Pro Tip: Use the Pomodoro Technique, which involves working in short, focused bursts (usually 25 minutes) followed by short breaks. This method helps maintain focus while preventing burnout.

10.4 Avoiding Burnout

Burnout is a state of chronic physical and emotional exhaustion caused by prolonged stress. It can lead to decreased motivation, reduced job performance, and even health problems. Preventing burnout requires proactive self-care, effective workload management, and recognizing the signs early.

10.4.1 Recognizing the Signs of Burnout

Burnout can develop gradually, so it's important to recognize the early warning signs and take steps to address them.

Common Signs of Burnout:
- Chronic Fatigue: You feel constantly tired, even after resting.
- Cynicism or Detachment: You feel emotionally distant from your work or colleagues and have lost enthusiasm for your job.
- Decreased Productivity: You struggle to complete tasks that used to be manageable and find it hard to concentrate.
- Physical Symptoms: Burnout can lead to physical symptoms such as headaches, stomachaches, and difficulty sleeping.

10.4.2 Strategies for Preventing Burnout

Preventing burnout requires maintaining a sustainable workload and practicing self-care. Here are a few strategies to help you avoid burnout:

- Take Regular Breaks: Make sure to take short breaks throughout the day, as well as longer breaks during weekends or vacations. Time away from work allows you to recharge and return with renewed energy.
- Delegate When Possible: Don't hesitate to delegate tasks to colleagues if you're feeling overwhelmed. Trying to do everything yourself can quickly lead to burnout.
- Set Realistic Goals: Avoid setting overly ambitious goals that require working long hours. Break large projects into manageable tasks and celebrate small wins along the way.
- Practice Mindfulness and Relaxation: Techniques such as meditation, deep breathing exercises, and yoga can help reduce stress and promote relaxation.

10.4.3 Seeking Support

Burnout can sometimes feel isolating, but seeking support from others can help you manage stress and find balance. Whether you're experiencing burnout symptoms or want to prevent them, connecting with others can provide perspective and relief.

How to Seek Support:

- Talk to Your Manager: If you're feeling overwhelmed at work, have a conversation with your manager about your workload. They may be able to help you prioritize tasks, delegate responsibilities, or adjust deadlines.
- Lean on Colleagues: Your coworkers can be a great source of support, especially if they're going through similar challenges. Don't hesitate to reach out for advice or share your experiences.
- Seek Professional Help: If burnout symptoms persist, consider seeking help from a counselor or therapist. Many companies offer Employee Assistance Programs (EAPs) that provide mental health support and resources.

Pro Tip: Don't wait until burnout is overwhelming before seeking support. Having regular check-ins with your manager or a trusted mentor can help prevent burnout by addressing stressors early on.

10.5 Integrating Self-Care into Your Routine

Maintaining a healthy work-life balance requires taking care of yourself, both physically and mentally. Self-care is the practice of nurturing your well-being through activities that promote relaxation, stress reduction, and personal fulfillment. Prioritizing self-care helps prevent burnout and supports long-term health.

10.5.1 Physical Self-Care

Physical health is closely tied to mental well-being, and taking care of your body is essential for maintaining energy and focus at work.

Ways to Practice Physical Self-Care:
- Exercise Regularly: Incorporate physical activity into your routine, whether it's going for a walk, hitting the gym, or practicing yoga. Exercise boosts endorphins, reduces stress, and improves overall health.
- Get Enough Sleep: Prioritize sleep by sticking to a consistent sleep schedule and creating a restful environment. Aim for 7-9 hours of quality sleep each night.
- Eat a Balanced Diet: Nourish your body with healthy, balanced meals that provide sustained energy throughout the day. Avoid excessive caffeine or sugar, which can lead to energy crashes.

10.5.2 Mental and Emotional Self-Care

Taking care of your mental and emotional well-being is just as important as physical self-care. Mental health practices can help you manage stress, stay focused, and improve your emotional resilience.

Ways to Practice Mental and Emotional Self-Care:
- Practice Mindfulness: Mindfulness techniques, such as meditation or deep breathing, help you stay present and reduce stress. Even a few minutes a day can make a big difference.
- Pursue Hobbies: Make time for hobbies and activities that bring you joy and relaxation. Whether it's reading, painting, cooking, or playing music, these activities allow you to recharge and disconnect from work.
- Set Aside "Me Time": Spend time alone doing things that relax and fulfill you, such as journaling, reflecting, or simply unwinding.

10.5.3 Social Self-Care

Humans are social creatures, and nurturing relationships with family, friends, and colleagues is essential for a balanced life. Social self-care involves maintaining connections with the people who support you.

Ways to Practice Social Self-Care:
- Stay Connected with Loved Ones: Make time to connect with family and friends, even during busy periods. Regular social interaction can reduce stress and improve emotional well-being.
- Build a Support Network: Surround yourself with people who support your goals and provide positive encouragement. This could be through family, friends, mentors, or professional networks.

- Participate in Social Activities: Engage in social activities outside of work, whether it's attending social events, joining clubs, or spending time with friends.

10.6 Balancing Personal Goals with Career Ambitions

Work-life balance isn't just about managing your work hours—it's about finding harmony between your personal aspirations and professional ambitions. Achieving balance requires you to dedicate time and energy to both areas in a way that supports long-term fulfillment.

10.6.1 Aligning Career Goals with Personal Values

A critical aspect of achieving work-life balance is ensuring that your career goals align with your personal values and long-term aspirations. When your work is aligned with your values, it feels more fulfilling and less like a drain on your personal life.

How to Align Your Goals:
- Reflect on Your Values: Take time to identify your core personal values (e.g., family, creativity, health, financial independence) and how they align with your career goals.
- Set Boundaries to Protect Your Values: If spending time with family is important to you, establish clear boundaries to ensure that work doesn't interfere with family life.
- Pursue Meaningful Work: Seek roles or projects that allow you to engage in work that aligns with your passions and personal values.

10.6.2 Making Time for Personal Growth

Just as you invest time in your professional growth, it's essential to dedicate time to personal growth. This includes pursuing personal goals, hobbies, and interests that enrich your life outside of work.

Ways to Make Time for Personal Growth:
- Schedule Personal Time: Just as you schedule meetings or tasks, schedule time for personal growth activities like reading, learning new skills, or pursuing creative interests.
- Take Breaks from Work: Use your vacation time, and don't feel guilty about taking time off to focus on yourself. A break from work can rejuvenate your mind and help you return more motivated.
- Balance Long-Term Goals: Set long-term personal goals (e.g., learning a new language, traveling, completing a passion project) and work toward them alongside your career goals.

Conclusion

Maintaining a healthy work-life balance is critical to both your professional success and personal well-being. Achieving this balance requires setting boundaries, managing your time effectively, and prioritizing self-care. By integrating these practices into your routine, you can prevent burnout, improve your job satisfaction, and ensure that your career ambitions are aligned with your personal values and goals. Remember, work-life balance is a dynamic process that requires constant attention and adjustment. Regularly check in with yourself to ensure that you're staying balanced and fulfilled in both your work and personal life.

Chapter 11: Navigating Career Transitions: Successfully Changing Careers, Industries, or Roles

As you progress through your career, there may come a time when you decide to make a change—whether it's moving into a new role, transitioning to a different industry, or pursuing an entirely new career path. Career transitions can be both exciting and challenging, requiring thoughtful planning, adaptability, and a willingness to step outside of your comfort zone. In this chapter, we will explore strategies for navigating career transitions successfully, including how to identify when it's time for a change, how to prepare for a new role or industry, and how to make a smooth transition without losing momentum in your career.

11.1 Identifying When It's Time for a Career Change

Before making any major career changes, it's important to evaluate whether you're truly ready for a transition. There are several signs that may indicate it's time to move on from your current role, industry, or career.

11.1.1 Signs It's Time for a Career Change

Here are some common indicators that it may be time to explore new career opportunities:

- **Lack of Fulfillment**: If you consistently feel unfulfilled in your work, or if your job no longer aligns with your personal values or passions, it may be a sign that you need to explore other options.
- **No Room for Growth**: If you've reached a plateau in your current role and see little opportunity for advancement or development, it may be time to consider a transition to a role with more growth potential.
- **Burnout**: Chronic stress, fatigue, and a feeling of being overwhelmed can be signs of burnout, which may indicate that a change in your work environment or role is needed.
- **Loss of Passion**: If you've lost interest in the work you're doing, or you're no longer excited by the challenges and opportunities in your field, a career change could reignite your passion.
- **Changing Interests**: As people grow and evolve, their interests and career goals may change. If you find yourself increasingly drawn to a different field or industry, it could be time to make a shift.

Pro Tip: Before making a drastic decision, take time to reflect on what specifically isn't working in your current role. Is it the job itself, the company culture, or something else? Identifying the root cause can help you make a more informed decision about your next steps.

11.1.2 Evaluating Your Readiness for Change

Once you've identified the signs that it may be time for a career change, it's important to assess your readiness. Making a successful transition requires both careful planning and the willingness to embrace uncertainty.

Questions to Ask Yourself:
- Am I clear about what I want in my next career move?: Do you know which direction you want to go in, or are you simply feeling the need for change? Clarifying your goals is essential before making any major decisions.
- Do I have the necessary skills or qualifications?: If you're transitioning into a new industry or role, consider whether you need additional training or education to be competitive in that field.
- Am I financially prepared for a potential transition?: Career transitions, especially when changing industries, may require a period of adjustment, including possible salary reductions. Assess your financial stability and plan accordingly.
- Am I open to learning and adapting?: A successful career transition often involves learning new skills, building new networks, and adapting to a different work culture. Are you prepared to embrace these challenges?

11.2 Planning for a Career Transition

Once you've determined that a career change is the right move, the next step is to develop a plan that will help you make a successful transition. This plan should include setting clear goals, identifying the skills you need, and networking with people in your desired field.

11.2.1 Setting Clear Goals

Whether you're looking to switch industries or transition to a new role within your current field, setting specific, measurable, achievable, relevant, and time-bound (SMART) goals will help guide your transition.

Examples of SMART Career Transition Goals:

Short-Term Goal: "Within the next six months, I will complete a certification program in digital marketing to prepare for a career shift into the field."

Long-Term Goal: "In the next two years, I will transition from a project management role in construction to a project management role in the tech industry by building relevant skills, networking with industry professionals, and applying to jobs."

By setting clear goals, you can break down the steps required for your transition and measure your progress along the way.

11.2.2 Building the Necessary Skills

If you're transitioning into a new role or industry, you may need to build new skills or enhance your current ones to be competitive. Research the qualifications and skills commonly required for your target role and identify any gaps in your experience.

How to Build New Skills:
- Online Learning: Platforms like Coursera, Udemy, LinkedIn Learning, and edX offer courses and certifications in a wide variety of fields. You can use these platforms to build technical skills, gain industry knowledge, or develop leadership capabilities.
- Certifications: Earning industry-recognized certifications can enhance your credibility and demonstrate your commitment to learning.
- On-the-Job Experience: If possible, take on new projects or responsibilities in your current role that align with the skills you want to develop.
- Volunteer or Freelance: If your current role doesn't offer opportunities to build the skills you need, consider volunteering or taking on freelance work to gain hands-on experience in your desired field.

Pro Tip: Keep a running list of the skills you acquire and projects you complete during this transition period. This will not only help you stay focused but will also provide valuable material for updating your resume or LinkedIn profile.

11.2.3 Networking in Your Desired Industry

Networking is a critical part of any career transition. By connecting with people in your desired industry, you can gain valuable insights into the field, learn about job opportunities, and build relationships with potential mentors or employers.

How to Network Effectively:

- Attend Industry Events: Conferences, webinars, and workshops related to your target industry can help you meet professionals who share your interests and can offer guidance.
- Leverage LinkedIn: Use LinkedIn to connect with people in your target industry. Send personalized connection requests and engage with their content to start building relationships.
- Join Professional Associations: Many industries have professional associations that offer networking events, job boards, and educational resources. Becoming an active member can help you expand your network.
- Request Informational Interviews: Informational interviews are a great way to learn about a new field while expanding your professional connections. Reach out to individuals in your desired industry and ask if they'd be willing to chat about their career experiences.

Example Informational Interview Request: "Hi [Name], I came across your profile and noticed that you've had an impressive career in [Industry/Field]. I'm currently exploring a career transition into this space and would love the opportunity to hear more about your journey and any advice you might have. Would you be open to a 15-minute chat at your convenience? Thank you for your time!"

11.3 Making a Smooth Transition

Making a successful career transition requires not only preparation but also adaptability during the transition period. From updating your resume to adjusting to a new work environment, there are several steps you can take to make the process smoother.

11.3.1 Updating Your Resume and LinkedIn Profile

As you transition to a new career or industry, your resume and LinkedIn profile should reflect your relevant skills, experiences, and qualifications.

How to Tailor Your Resume for a Career Transition:
- Highlight Transferable Skills: Emphasize skills that are applicable across industries, such as project management, leadership, communication, or problem-solving.
- Focus on Accomplishments: Use measurable accomplishments to demonstrate your impact in previous roles, even if those roles were in a different industry.
- Include Relevant Certifications or Training: If you've completed any certifications or training related to your new field, be sure to feature them prominently on your resume.
- Use Keywords from Job Descriptions: Incorporate keywords from job postings in your desired field to ensure that your resume aligns with the qualifications employers are seeking.

Pro Tip: Use LinkedIn to showcase your career transition journey. Update your headline and summary to reflect your new career goals, and share posts or articles related to your desired industry to demonstrate your knowledge and engagement.

11.3.2 Adjusting to a New Role or Industry

When you start a new role or enter a new industry, it's important to be patient with yourself as you adjust. There will be a learning curve, and it may take time to fully acclimate to the new environment.

Tips for Succeeding in a New Role:
- Ask Questions: Don't be afraid to ask questions as you learn the ropes in your new role. This shows your willingness to learn and helps you avoid mistakes.
- Seek Out a Mentor: Find someone in your new role or industry who can offer guidance and support during your transition. A mentor can help you navigate challenges and accelerate your learning process.

- Stay Open to Feedback: Be open to constructive feedback from colleagues and supervisors. This feedback will help you grow in your new role and ensure that you're on the right track.
- Embrace Continuous Learning: Continue learning and improving your skills even after you've made the transition. Industries evolve quickly, and staying informed will help you remain competitive.

11.3.3 Managing Uncertainty During a Career Change

Career transitions can come with uncertainty and self-doubt, especially if you are moving into an entirely new field or role. Managing this uncertainty is key to maintaining your confidence and motivation throughout the process. It's normal to feel unsure at times, but with the right mindset and support, you can navigate these challenges successfully.

Tips for Managing Uncertainty:
- Embrace a Growth Mindset: View your career transition as an opportunity to learn and grow rather than as a risk. With a growth mindset, you can see challenges as learning experiences that will make you stronger and more adaptable in the long run.
- Focus on What You Can Control: While certain aspects of the career transition process—such as timing or specific job offers—may be outside of your control, focus on what you can influence. Continue building your skills, networking, and seeking out opportunities.
- Break It Down into Small Steps: Large career changes can feel overwhelming, but breaking down the process into smaller, manageable steps can make it feel less daunting. Focus on one task at a time, such as completing a certification or reaching out to a new contact, rather than trying to tackle everything at once.
- Maintain a Support System: Surround yourself with supportive friends, family, mentors, or colleagues who can offer encouragement and perspective during your transition. Discussing your concerns with others can help alleviate anxiety and provide valuable insights.

Pro Tip: Keep a journal to track your progress, setbacks, and reflections during your career transition. This can serve as both a motivational tool and a record of your journey, helping you see how far you've come.

11.4 Overcoming Common Career Transition Challenges

Career transitions come with their own set of challenges, from dealing with rejection to managing imposter syndrome. By recognizing these challenges in advance, you can develop strategies to overcome them and stay focused on your goals.

11.4.1 Dealing with Rejection

Rejection is a normal part of any job search, but it can be especially disheartening during a career transition when you're stepping into unfamiliar territory. It's important to stay resilient and not let rejection derail your progress.

How to Handle Rejection:
- Reframe Rejection: Instead of seeing rejection as a personal failure, view it as a learning opportunity. Ask for feedback when possible and use that information to improve your approach in future applications.
- Stay Persistent: Remember that career transitions often take time, and rejection is part of the process. Stay focused on your long-term goals and keep applying to opportunities that align with your career aspirations.
- Take Breaks When Needed: Job searches and career transitions can be exhausting, so don't hesitate to take breaks when needed to recharge. A fresh perspective can help you approach your next application or interview with renewed energy.

11.4.2 Managing Imposter Syndrome

Imposter syndrome—feeling like you don't belong or aren't qualified for a new role—is common during career transitions. Even when you've put in the work to prepare for your new role, self-doubt can creep in.

Tips for Overcoming Imposter Syndrome:
- Acknowledge Your Accomplishments: Take time to reflect on the skills, experiences, and achievements that have brought you to this point. Remind yourself that you've earned your place in your new role or industry.
- Seek Validation from Trusted Sources: If you're doubting your abilities, talk to a mentor or trusted colleague who can provide honest feedback and remind you of your strengths.
- Focus on Continuous Improvement: Rather than trying to be perfect right away, focus on learning and growing in your new role. Every new opportunity is a chance to improve your skills and gain more confidence.

Pro Tip: Keep a "success journal" where you record your accomplishments and positive feedback. Reviewing this journal during moments of self-doubt can help reinforce your confidence.

11.4.3 Balancing Financial Stability During a Transition

Career transitions, especially when changing industries, may involve a temporary reduction in income or a longer job search period. It's important to manage your finances carefully during this time to reduce stress.

Financial Tips for Career Transitions:
- Create a Budget: Outline your monthly expenses and determine how much you need to save to cover essential costs during your transition. Cut back on non-essential spending when possible to reduce financial pressure.
- Build an Emergency Fund: If you anticipate a period of unemployment or a lower salary, try to save an emergency fund that covers three to six months of living expenses. This will provide a safety net while you adjust to your new career.
- Explore Temporary or Freelance Work: If your job search is taking longer than expected, consider taking on temporary or freelance work in your current field to maintain financial stability while you continue pursuing your career goals.

11.5 Measuring Success in Your Career Transition

Success in a career transition looks different for everyone, but it's important to track your progress and celebrate milestones along the way. Whether you're transitioning into a new industry, role, or level of responsibility, recognizing your achievements will help you stay motivated.

11.5.1 Setting Transition Milestones

To stay on track during your transition, set specific milestones that you can work toward. These milestones will give you a sense of accomplishment and help you measure your progress.

Examples of Career Transition Milestones:
- Completing a key certification or training program.
- Gaining your first freelance client or landing your first job interview in a new industry.
- Expanding your professional network by attending a certain number of industry events or connecting with new contacts.
- Successfully managing your first project in a new role.

11.5.2 Reflecting on Your Progress

Regularly reflect on your career transition journey and assess how far you've come. Take note of the challenges you've overcome, the skills you've developed, and the new opportunities you've embraced.

Reflection Questions:
- What new skills have I developed during this transition?
- What challenges have I successfully navigated, and how did I handle them?
- What lessons have I learned about myself and my career goals?

11.5.3 Celebrating Small Wins

Career transitions can be long and complex, so it's important to celebrate small wins along the way. These small victories, such as completing a course, acing an interview, or expanding your network, contribute to your overall success.

How to Celebrate Wins:
- Treat Yourself: Reward yourself with something small, like a nice dinner, a new book, or a weekend getaway, whenever you reach a significant milestone.
- Share Your Success: Don't be afraid to share your accomplishments with friends, family, or professional connections. Their support and encouragement can help keep you motivated.

Conclusion

Navigating a career transition, whether it's changing industries, roles, or levels of responsibility, requires careful planning, resilience, and adaptability. By setting clear goals, building the necessary skills, and actively networking, you can position yourself for success in your new career. Managing the challenges of a career transition—such as rejection, imposter syndrome, and financial uncertainty—will help you stay focused and confident throughout the process. Remember to celebrate your progress along the way, as each small step brings you closer to your ultimate career goals.

Chapter 12: Developing a Personal and Professional Brand: Building and Maintaining a Strong Reputation

In today's competitive job market, developing a strong personal and professional brand is essential for long-term career success. Your personal brand is how others perceive you—it's your reputation, your unique set of skills, and the value you bring to the workplace. Whether you're a recent graduate starting your career, or a seasoned professional looking to advance, cultivating and managing your personal brand can open doors to new opportunities, build trust with colleagues and clients, and position you as a leader in your field.

In this chapter, we'll cover how to define your personal brand, establish a professional online presence, and maintain your brand over time. We'll also explore how to leverage your brand to advance your career and create meaningful relationships in your industry.

12.1 Understanding Personal Branding

Personal branding is the process of marketing yourself—your skills, experience, and personality—as a brand. It's about shaping how others perceive you and ensuring that your professional identity aligns with your career goals. Your brand should reflect your strengths, values, and what sets you apart from others.

12.1.1 Why Personal Branding Matters

Your personal brand is your professional identity, and it plays a critical role in your career development.

A strong personal brand can:
- Attract Opportunities: A well-defined brand helps potential employers, clients, and collaborators understand what you bring to the table. This can lead to new job offers, partnerships, and networking opportunities.
- Build Credibility: A strong brand positions you as a trusted expert in your field. By consistently showcasing your knowledge and skills, you build credibility and trust with your audience.
- Enhance Career Progression: Whether you're seeking a promotion or transitioning into a new role, a strong personal brand can help you stand out from your peers and demonstrate your leadership potential.

12.1.2 The Key Elements of Personal Branding

Your personal brand is made up of several key elements that work together to create your professional identity.

These elements include:
- Skills and Expertise: The knowledge and technical skills that set you apart from others in your industry.
- Values and Personality: Your personal values, work ethic, and personality traits, which influence how you interact with others and approach your work.
- Experience and Accomplishments: The projects, roles, and achievements that showcase your contributions and impact.
- Unique Selling Proposition (USP): The specific value you offer that differentiates you from others in your field.

Pro Tip: Your personal brand should be authentic—don't try to be someone you're not. The most effective brands are built on genuine strengths, values, and passions.

12.2 Defining Your Personal Brand

Before you can build a strong personal brand, you need to clearly define what you want that brand to represent. This involves reflecting on your skills, values, and career goals, and then crafting a brand statement that summarizes who you are and what you bring to the table.

12.2.1 Self-Assessment

To define your personal brand, start with a self-assessment. Reflect on your strengths, passions, and the unique value you bring to your work.

Questions to Ask Yourself:
- What are my key strengths and skills?: Identify the technical and soft skills that you excel at and enjoy using in your work.
- What am I passionate about?: Consider the types of projects or roles that excite and motivate you.
- What are my career goals?: Think about where you want to go in your career and how your personal brand can support those goals.
- What sets me apart from others?: Determine what makes you unique in your field—whether it's a specific skill set, a particular way of solving problems, or a perspective that adds value.

Pro Tip: Ask colleagues, mentors, or trusted friends for feedback on how they perceive your strengths and skills. This external perspective can help you gain clarity on your brand.

12.2.2 Crafting Your Brand Statement

Once you've completed your self-assessment, use that information to craft a personal brand statement. This statement should be a concise summary of who you are, what you do, and what sets you apart. Your brand statement serves as the foundation for your online presence, resume, and professional interactions.

Example Brand Statement: "I am a strategic marketing professional with expertise in digital content creation and data-driven campaigns. I'm passionate about helping businesses grow their online presence through creative storytelling and innovative marketing strategies. My unique approach combines creativity with analytics, allowing me to deliver measurable results for my clients."

Your brand statement should be clear, compelling, and aligned with your career goals. It should also be adaptable so that you can tailor it to different audiences and situations.

12.3 Building an Online Presence

In today's digital world, your online presence plays a significant role in your personal brand. Potential employers, clients, and colleagues often research you online before meeting or working with you, so it's important to present a consistent, professional image across all platforms.

12.3.1 Optimizing Your LinkedIn Profile

LinkedIn is the premier platform for building a professional online presence. It's not only a place to showcase your resume but also a tool for networking, thought leadership, and personal branding.

Tips for Optimizing Your LinkedIn Profile:
- Profile Picture: Use a professional, high-quality headshot that reflects your personal brand. Avoid casual or overly stylized photos.
- Headline: Your LinkedIn headline should reflect your brand statement. It should clearly communicate what you do and what sets you apart.
- Summary: Write a compelling summary that highlights your skills, experience, and career goals. Use this space to tell your story and explain how you add value in your field.
- Experience and Accomplishments: List your relevant work experience, but focus on measurable achievements rather than just job descriptions. Use bullet points to make your accomplishments easy to read.
- Skills and Endorsements: Highlight the key skills that align with your brand. Encourage colleagues to endorse you for these skills to build credibility.
- Engage with Content: Share articles, post updates, and comment on industry topics to demonstrate your knowledge and stay active in your network.

Pro Tip: Consistently engage with your LinkedIn network by liking, sharing, or commenting on posts relevant to your field. This increases your visibility and helps build relationships.

12.3.2 Creating a Personal Website

A personal website is an excellent tool for showcasing your portfolio, sharing your expertise, and controlling your online presence. While LinkedIn is essential, a website allows you to present a more personalized and comprehensive picture of your brand.

What to Include on a Personal Website:
- About Me: A page that summarizes your personal brand, including your background, skills, values, and career goals.
- Portfolio: Showcase examples of your work, such as case studies, projects, or client testimonials. Include images, videos, or documents that highlight your achievements.
- Blog or Thought Leadership: Consider writing blog posts or articles on topics related to your field. This demonstrates your expertise and positions you as a thought leader.
- Contact Information: Provide a way for potential employers, clients, or collaborators to get in touch with you, whether through email or a contact form.

12.3.3 Managing Your Online Reputation

Beyond LinkedIn and your personal website, it's important to be mindful of your overall online presence. Ensure that your social media accounts and any public profiles align with your professional brand.

Tips for Managing Your Online Reputation:
- Google Yourself: Regularly search your name online to see what potential employers or clients might find. If necessary, update or remove any content that doesn't align with your personal brand.
- Consistent Messaging: Ensure that your personal brand messaging is consistent across all platforms. Whether it's your LinkedIn, personal website, or Twitter account, your online presence should reflect the same professional identity.
- Engage Professionally: If you're active on platforms like Twitter, Instagram, or Facebook, maintain a level of professionalism. Avoid sharing content that could be seen as unprofessional or polarizing unless it's directly related to your brand.

12.4 Maintaining and Evolving Your Brand

Building a personal brand is not a one-time event—it's an ongoing process that requires attention and adaptation. As your career grows and evolves, so should your brand. Continuously refining and updating your brand helps ensure that it remains relevant and aligned with your career goals.

12.4.1 Regularly Updating Your Brand

As you gain new skills, take on new projects, and achieve new milestones in your career, be sure to update your brand to reflect these changes.

When to Update Your Brand:
- New Role or Promotion: If you've transitioned into a new role or received a promotion, update your online presence, resume, and brand statement to reflect your new responsibilities.
- New Skills or Certifications: Add any new skills, certifications, or professional development achievements to your online profiles and personal brand materials.
- Shifting Career Goals: If your career goals or focus areas have changed, ensure that your brand messaging aligns with your new direction.

12.4.2 Adapting to Industry Trends

Your personal brand should evolve alongside your industry. Stay informed about trends and advancements in your field and adapt your brand to reflect the latest skills and knowledge.

How to Stay Relevant:
- Continuous Learning: Pursue ongoing professional development through courses, certifications, or training programs that keep you up to date with industry trends.
- Thought Leadership: Share your insights on industry trends through blog posts, LinkedIn articles, or presentations. By contributing to the conversation in your industry, you position yourself as a thought leader and demonstrate your expertise to a wider audience.

Ways to Share Thought Leadership:

- Write Articles or Blog Posts: Regularly share your thoughts on industry trends, challenges, or innovations. This not only showcases your knowledge but also helps build your online presence.
- Speak at Conferences or Webinars: Seek out opportunities to speak at industry events or participate in webinars. Public speaking builds credibility and can expand your professional network.
- Create Educational Content: Consider creating tutorials, how-to guides, or educational videos that can help others in your field learn new skills or stay informed about emerging trends.

12.4.3 Building a Strong Network to Support Your Brand

Your personal brand is strengthened by the relationships you cultivate. A strong professional network can help you build credibility, gain visibility, and open doors to new opportunities. Networking should be an ongoing part of maintaining and evolving your brand.

How to Build and Maintain a Professional Network:
- Engage with Industry Peers: Attend industry events, conferences, and webinars to meet and connect with other professionals. Follow up with connections to build meaningful relationships.
- Use LinkedIn for Networking: Regularly connect with new contacts in your field and engage with their content. Join relevant LinkedIn groups to participate in discussions and share your insights.
- Offer Value to Your Network: Networking isn't just about what you can get from others. Look for opportunities to provide value, whether through sharing resources, offering advice, or connecting people in your network.
- Stay Connected: Keep in touch with your network through regular check-ins. Send congratulatory messages for achievements, share interesting articles, or offer support when needed.

12.5 Leveraging Your Brand for Career Advancement

A strong personal and professional brand can help you stand out in a competitive job market and advance your career. By actively promoting your brand, you can attract new opportunities, gain recognition, and position yourself for leadership roles.

12.5.1 Positioning Yourself for Promotions

If you're looking to advance within your current organization, your personal brand can be a key factor in positioning yourself for a promotion. By consistently demonstrating your value and showcasing your leadership potential, you can stand out as a candidate for advancement.

How to Position Yourself for Promotion:
- Align Your Brand with Company Goals: Ensure that your personal brand aligns with your organization's values and long-term goals. Show how your skills and contributions support the company's vision.
- Showcase Leadership Skills: Even if you're not in a formal leadership role, look for opportunities to take the lead on projects, mentor colleagues, or propose new initiatives. Demonstrating leadership skills is key to advancing your career.
- Consistently Deliver Results: Build a reputation for excellence by consistently delivering high-quality work and meeting or exceeding expectations. Use measurable results to back up your achievements when discussing career advancement with your supervisor.

12.5.2 Attracting New Job Opportunities

Your personal brand can also help you attract new job opportunities, whether through recruiters, colleagues, or industry contacts. By consistently showcasing your expertise, you increase your chances of being noticed by hiring managers or potential clients.

How to Attract Job Opportunities with Your Brand:

- Be Active on LinkedIn: Recruiters often search LinkedIn for potential candidates, so having an optimized and active profile can increase your visibility. Regularly engage with content, update your profile with accomplishments, and signal your interest in new opportunities.
- Promote Your Work: Use your website, portfolio, or social media platforms to showcase examples of your work. Whether it's case studies, design projects, or marketing campaigns, providing tangible evidence of your impact can attract employers and clients.
- Expand Your Reach: Don't limit yourself to just your immediate network. Consider writing guest posts on industry blogs, speaking at external events, or contributing to publications that reach a wider audience.

12.5.3 Leveraging Your Brand for Freelance or Entrepreneurial Ventures

For professionals interested in freelancing or starting their own business, personal branding is especially important. Your brand serves as your calling card, and how you present yourself can directly influence the clients and opportunities you attract.

How to Leverage Your Brand for Freelancing or Entrepreneurship:
- Clearly Define Your Niche: Focus your brand on a specific area of expertise where you can offer unique value. Defining your niche helps potential clients understand what sets you apart from other freelancers or businesses.
- Showcase Client Success Stories: Highlight testimonials, case studies, and examples of how you've helped clients achieve their goals. Positive reviews and case studies build trust with potential clients.
- Market Yourself Actively: Use social media, your personal website, and industry networks to actively promote your services. Regularly share updates about your work, success stories, and availability for new projects.
- Build Long-Term Relationships: Freelancers and entrepreneurs often rely on repeat clients or referrals, so building strong, long-term relationships is critical. Deliver excellent service and maintain regular communication with your clients.

Conclusion

Developing a strong personal and professional brand is a powerful tool for advancing your career, attracting new opportunities, and building a lasting reputation in your industry. By defining your brand, building an online presence, and maintaining your brand as you grow, you can establish yourself as a leader and trusted expert in your field. Whether you're seeking a promotion, exploring new job opportunities, or building your own business, your personal brand will play a key role in your success.

Remember, branding is an ongoing process that requires attention and adaptation as your career evolves. Stay consistent, remain authentic, and continuously invest in your brand to ensure it remains aligned with your long-term career goals.

Chapter 13: Navigating Workplace Politics: Building Positive Relationships and Advancing with Integrity

Workplace politics is an unavoidable aspect of professional life, and knowing how to navigate it effectively can significantly impact your career. While office politics often have negative connotations, they are not inherently bad—understanding and managing workplace dynamics can help you build strong relationships, position yourself for success, and maintain your professional integrity. The key is to engage in workplace politics in a way that is ethical, constructive, and aligned with your values.

In this chapter, we'll explore how to identify workplace dynamics, build strategic relationships, avoid common political pitfalls, and advance your career while maintaining your integrity and credibility.

13.1 Understanding Workplace Politics

Workplace politics refers to the complex network of power dynamics, relationships, and influence within an organization. Politics can influence decision-making, career advancement, resource allocation, and more. Learning how to navigate these dynamics with professionalism is essential to thriving in any organization.

13.1.1 The Role of Power and Influence

In any workplace, different individuals or groups hold varying degrees of power and influence. Power may come from an official position or title, but it can also come from informal sources such as expertise, personal relationships, or the ability to influence others.

Types of Power in the Workplace:
- Positional Power: Authority that comes from one's role or title within the organization. Managers, executives, and team leaders often have positional power.
- Expert Power: Power that stems from specialized knowledge, skills, or expertise. Individuals with deep knowledge in a particular area can wield influence, even without a formal leadership title.
- Relationship Power: Power derived from personal relationships, networks, and alliances. Those who are well-connected within the organization may have greater influence over decisions.
- Personal Power: Power that comes from personal traits such as charisma, confidence, and communication skills. Individuals with strong personal power can influence others through their personality.

Understanding the sources of power in your organization can help you navigate workplace dynamics more effectively.

13.1.2 Identifying Key Stakeholders

Key stakeholders in the workplace are individuals who hold influence over your career and projects. These stakeholders may be decision-makers, mentors, or influential colleagues. Identifying who holds influence can help you build strategic relationships and better position yourself for success.

How to Identify Key Stakeholders:
- Organizational Structure: Look at the organizational hierarchy to identify individuals in leadership roles who influence decision-making in your department or across the company.
- Informal Leaders: Some colleagues may hold informal influence through their relationships, knowledge, or ability to guide others. These individuals are often highly respected by peers and leadership.
- Cross-Departmental Connections: Don't limit your focus to just your immediate team—stakeholders from other departments, such as HR, finance, or IT, may have a significant impact on your projects and career.

Pro Tip: Once you've identified key stakeholders, observe how they interact with others. Understanding their communication styles, priorities, and decision-making processes can help you build more effective relationships.

13.2 Building Strategic Relationships

Positive workplace relationships are critical for navigating office politics and advancing your career. Strategic relationships provide you with support, mentorship, and access to opportunities, while helping you build a reputation as a team player and leader.

13.2.1 Cultivating Allies

Allies are colleagues who support your goals and advocate for you when opportunities arise. Cultivating allies in different areas of the organization can help you expand your influence and ensure you have a network of support.

How to Cultivate Allies:
- Build Trust: Trust is the foundation of strong professional relationships. Be reliable, follow through on commitments, and communicate openly with your colleagues.
- Offer Support: Helping others succeed fosters goodwill and can lead to reciprocal support. Offer assistance on projects, share knowledge, or provide feedback to colleagues when appropriate.
- Stay Collaborative: Collaboration is key to building positive relationships. Avoid being overly competitive or self-serving, and instead focus on working together to achieve shared goals.

13.2.2 Finding Mentors and Sponsors

Mentors and sponsors play a crucial role in career development by offering guidance, advocating for your advancement, and helping you navigate workplace politics. While mentors provide advice and support, sponsors actively champion your career and help you secure opportunities.

How to Find a Mentor:
- Identify Experienced Colleagues: Look for individuals within your organization or industry who have experience in areas you want to grow. A mentor with a background similar to your desired career path can offer valuable insights.
- Seek Formal Mentorship Programs: Many organizations offer formal mentorship programs where you can be paired with senior professionals for guidance.
- Reach Out for Informational Meetings: If a mentorship program doesn't exist, consider asking an experienced colleague for an informational meeting to discuss career advice. Over time, this relationship can evolve into mentorship.

How to Find a Sponsor:
- Look for Influential Leaders: Sponsors are typically senior leaders or individuals with significant influence within the organization. Identify potential sponsors who have a track record of helping others advance.
- Demonstrate Your Value: Sponsors invest their reputation by advocating for you, so it's important to demonstrate your value through high performance and results. Show that you're reliable, capable, and ambitious.
- Build Relationships Over Time: A sponsorship relationship is often built over time. Focus on delivering strong work, building rapport with potential sponsors, and expressing your career aspirations clearly.

13.2.3 Networking Across Departments

Cross-departmental networking is essential for building a broad base of support and influence within your organization. By networking with colleagues in different areas, you can gain new perspectives, collaborate on projects, and increase your visibility across the company.

Ways to Network Across Departments:
- Participate in Company Events: Attend company-wide events, training sessions, and social gatherings to meet colleagues from other departments.
- Join Cross-Functional Teams: If your company has cross-functional teams or project groups, volunteer to participate. This gives you the opportunity to work with colleagues from different areas and build relationships outside your immediate team.
- Seek Out Informal Interactions: Networking doesn't always have to be formal. Take advantage of informal interactions—such as lunch breaks, coffee chats, or casual conversations—to build connections.

Pro Tip: Networking across departments not only expands your influence but also helps you gain a more comprehensive understanding of the organization's operations and goals.

13.3 Managing Conflicts and Power Struggles

Conflicts and power struggles are inevitable in any workplace, but how you handle them can affect your reputation and career advancement. Navigating these situations with diplomacy and professionalism is key to maintaining positive relationships while avoiding damaging office politics.

13.3.1 Handling Conflicts Professionally

Conflicts can arise from differences in opinions, personalities, or goals. Rather than avoiding or escalating conflicts, effective professionals approach them constructively to find a resolution that benefits all parties.

Steps for Handling Workplace Conflicts:
1. Stay Calm and Objective: When conflicts arise, remain calm and avoid reacting emotionally. Take a step back to assess the situation objectively before responding.
2. Listen to Understand: Make an effort to understand the other person's perspective. Listen actively and acknowledge their concerns, even if you don't agree with them.
3. Focus on Solutions: Instead of dwelling on the problem, shift the conversation toward finding a solution. Look for common ground and propose compromises that satisfy both parties.
4. Seek Mediation if Needed: If you're unable to resolve a conflict on your own, consider involving a neutral third party, such as HR or a manager, to help mediate the situation.

Pro Tip: After a conflict is resolved, follow up with the other party to ensure that the solution is working for both sides. This demonstrates your commitment to maintaining a positive working relationship.

13.3.2 Avoiding Negative Office Politics

Negative office politics—such as gossip, manipulation, or backstabbing—can create a toxic work environment and damage your reputation. It's important to stay above these behaviors and engage in politics ethically and professionally.

How to Avoid Negative Politics:
- Don't Engage in Gossip: Avoid participating in office gossip or speaking negatively about colleagues. Gossip can erode trust and create divisions within teams.
- Maintain Integrity: Be honest and transparent in your actions. Avoid manipulating situations for personal gain or undermining others to get ahead.

- Focus on Collaboration: Rather than viewing colleagues as competition, focus on building collaborative relationships. A cooperative approach fosters a positive team environment and reduces the likelihood of negative politics.

13.3.3 Managing Power Struggles

Power struggles occur when individuals or groups compete for control, resources, or influence. Navigating power struggles requires tact, diplomacy, and a focus on shared goals rather than personal agendas.

How to Manage Power Struggles:
- Stay Neutral When Possible: If you're not directly involved in a power struggle, avoid taking sides. Stay focused on your work and maintain professionalism with all parties.
- Find Common Ground: When you're involved in a power struggle, look for areas of mutual interest or shared goals that can help de-escalate the situation.
- Keep the Focus on the Organization's Success: Shift the conversation away from personal agendas and refocus on the organization's broader goals. This can help defuse tensions and align everyone's efforts toward a common objective.

13.4 Advancing Your Career with Integrity

While it's important to be strategic in navigating workplace politics, it's equally important to maintain your integrity. Advancing your career through ethical means ensures that you build a reputation based on trust, professionalism, and respect.

13.4.1 Leading with Integrity

Leading with integrity means acting in accordance with your values and ethical standards, even when faced with difficult choices. Integrity is one of the most valuable qualities in a professional, as it fosters trust, builds credibility, and sets you apart as a reliable leader.

How to Lead with Integrity:
- Be Honest and Transparent: Always communicate openly and honestly with your colleagues and supervisors. Transparency helps build trust and ensures that others view you as someone who can be relied upon to speak the truth, even when it's difficult.
- Hold Yourself Accountable: Take responsibility for your actions, both positive and negative. If you make a mistake, own it and work to correct the issue, rather than shifting blame to others.
- Treat Everyone with Respect: Show respect to colleagues at all levels of the organization. Avoid favoritism and ensure that your decisions are fair and consistent.

- Uphold Ethical Standards: In situations where you are tempted to take shortcuts or engage in behavior that might benefit you in the short term, prioritize long-term success and your ethical principles.

13.4.2 Navigating Promotions and Career Advancements Ethically

When seeking a promotion or career advancement, it's important to balance ambition with professionalism. Navigating the political landscape to secure opportunities is part of career progression, but it's essential to do so without compromising your integrity.

How to Seek Promotions Ethically:
- Highlight Your Contributions: When pursuing a promotion, focus on your accomplishments and how they have benefited the company. Use data to back up your claims, showing measurable results from your work.
- Advocate for Yourself with Professionalism: When advocating for a promotion, avoid disparaging colleagues or competitors. Focus on your own achievements rather than comparing yourself to others.
- Build Genuine Relationships: Networking and building relationships are critical to advancing in your career, but these relationships should be based on mutual respect, not opportunism. Avoid using relationships solely for personal gain.
- Ask for Constructive Feedback: If you are not selected for a promotion, ask for feedback on areas for improvement. This demonstrates your commitment to growth and helps you prepare for future opportunities.

13.4.3 Balancing Ambition with Team Success

While career advancement is important, it's essential to balance personal ambition with the success of your team and organization. Helping others succeed and contributing to team goals will not only benefit the organization but will also enhance your reputation as a team player and leader.

How to Balance Ambition and Collaboration:
- Share Credit for Successes: When your team achieves success, make sure to acknowledge the contributions of others. Sharing credit builds trust and goodwill, while also positioning you as a leader who values collaboration.
- Support the Growth of Your Colleagues: Helping others develop their skills and advance in their careers can strengthen your team and create a positive work environment. Be open to mentoring and supporting your colleagues.
- Focus on Collective Wins: While individual achievements are important, focus on how your personal goals align with the broader goals of your team or department. Demonstrating that you are committed to the success of the organization will position you as a leader who can be trusted with greater responsibility.

13.5 Managing Office Politics in Remote or Hybrid Work Environments

With the rise of remote and hybrid work models, office politics have evolved, and managing relationships from a distance presents unique challenges. In these environments, building and maintaining strong professional relationships requires intentional communication and a proactive approach.

13.5.1 Building Relationships in a Remote Setting

In a remote work environment, it's easy to feel disconnected from colleagues, which can make navigating workplace politics more difficult. Proactively building relationships with your team members and stakeholders is essential for staying engaged and influential.

How to Build Relationships Remotely:
- Schedule Regular Check-Ins: Make time for virtual one-on-one meetings with key colleagues and stakeholders to maintain rapport and stay informed about ongoing projects and developments.
- Use Collaborative Tools: Take advantage of collaborative platforms such as Slack, Microsoft Teams, or Zoom to stay in regular communication with your team. Be active in group chats, video calls, and collaborative documents to remain visible and engaged.
- Attend Virtual Social Events: Participate in virtual team-building events, happy hours, or other informal gatherings that provide an opportunity to connect with colleagues on a personal level.

13.5.2 Managing Conflicts in a Remote Environment

Conflicts can still arise in a remote or hybrid work setting, but resolving them may require different strategies. Without face-to-face interaction, miscommunications are more likely to occur, making it essential to approach conflicts with extra care.

How to Manage Remote Conflicts:
- Address Issues Promptly: Don't let conflicts fester in a remote environment. Address issues as soon as they arise by scheduling a virtual meeting to discuss concerns.
- Communicate Clearly and Respectfully: In a remote setting, communication can be easily misinterpreted. Make an effort to communicate clearly, and use respectful language to prevent misunderstandings.
- Focus on Solutions: Just as in an in-person setting, focus on finding a solution rather than assigning blame. Encourage open dialogue and listen carefully to the other person's perspective.

13.5.3 Navigating Virtual Team Dynamics

Remote work can sometimes blur team dynamics, making it more difficult to understand who holds influence and how decisions are made. Paying attention to virtual team interactions and staying engaged in meetings can help you navigate these dynamics more effectively.

How to Navigate Virtual Team Dynamics:
- Observe Meeting Dynamics: In virtual meetings, pay attention to who speaks most frequently, who leads conversations, and who makes key decisions. This can give you insight into the power dynamics of your remote team.
- Be Proactive in Virtual Meetings: Ensure that you actively participate in virtual meetings by sharing your ideas, asking questions, and offering solutions. Being visible in virtual settings helps establish your presence and influence.
- Develop Cross-Functional Connections: Even in a remote setting, it's important to build relationships across departments. Reach out to colleagues in other areas of the organization to broaden your network and stay informed about cross-functional initiatives.

Conclusion

Navigating workplace politics is a necessary part of career success, but it doesn't have to compromise your integrity or professionalism. By understanding workplace dynamics, building strategic relationships, managing conflicts effectively, and advancing your career with honesty and transparency, you can thrive in any organizational environment. Whether you're working in an office or navigating a remote or hybrid workplace, the same principles of collaboration, trust, and ethical behavior apply.

Chapter 14: Managing Leadership Transitions: Succeeding as a New Leader

Transitioning into a leadership role is a significant milestone in any career. Whether you've been promoted within your current organization, taken on a leadership position at a new company, or are starting your own team, this new responsibility requires you to develop a different set of skills and perspectives. Becoming an effective leader involves not only managing your own work but also guiding and motivating others, setting strategic goals, and making key decisions that impact the team's success.

In this chapter, we'll explore how to navigate the transition into leadership, build trust with your team, establish your leadership style, and set yourself up for long-term success in your new role.

14.1 Preparing for a Leadership Role

Before stepping into a leadership position, it's important to prepare yourself mentally and professionally for the new responsibilities. Leadership requires a shift in focus—from managing your own performance to managing the performance and well-being of an entire team. By preparing in advance, you can ensure a smoother transition and avoid common leadership challenges.

14.1.1 Understanding Your New Responsibilities

One of the first steps in transitioning to a leadership role is gaining a clear understanding of your new responsibilities. Leadership goes beyond managing tasks—it involves setting a vision, empowering your team, and ensuring that the team's efforts align with the organization's goals.

Key Leadership Responsibilities:
- Setting Direction: As a leader, you'll be responsible for defining the team's goals and aligning them with the broader objectives of the organization.
- Motivating and Developing the Team: Leaders play a critical role in motivating their team members, providing mentorship, and helping them grow professionally.
- Making Strategic Decisions: Leadership involves making decisions that affect the direction of the team, the allocation of resources, and the prioritization of tasks.
- Managing Conflicts and Challenges: You'll be responsible for addressing conflicts within the team, resolving problems, and maintaining a positive work environment.

14.1.2 Developing a Leadership Mindset

Shifting from an individual contributor to a leader requires a change in mindset. While individual contributors focus on their own tasks and performance, leaders must take a broader view of the team's success. Developing a leadership mindset involves learning to see the bigger picture, taking ownership of team outcomes, and adopting a people-first approach.

Steps to Develop a Leadership Mindset:
- Focus on the Team's Success: Rather than measuring your success solely by your own achievements, shift your focus to the team's collective success. Recognize that your role is to enable others to perform at their best.
- Embrace Accountability: Leaders are responsible for the team's performance and outcomes. Be prepared to take accountability for both successes and challenges, and work proactively to address issues.
- Cultivate Empathy and Emotional Intelligence: Leadership requires understanding the needs and motivations of your team members. Develop your emotional intelligence by practicing empathy, active listening, and effective communication.
- Adopt a Long-Term Perspective: Leaders must think strategically and consider the long-term impact of their decisions. As you step into your role, begin looking at how short-term actions align with long-term goals.

14.2 Building Trust with Your Team

Trust is the foundation of effective leadership. Without trust, it's difficult to motivate your team, foster collaboration, or achieve collective goals. Building trust takes time, but it's essential for creating a positive work environment and establishing your credibility as a leader.

14.2.1 Building Relationships with Team Members

As a new leader, one of your first priorities should be building strong relationships with your team members. Get to know each individual, understand their strengths and motivations, and create an open line of communication.

Ways to Build Relationships:
- Schedule One-on-One Meetings: Meet with each team member individually to learn more about their roles, challenges, and career goals. This shows that you value their input and are committed to supporting their development.
- Listen Actively: Practice active listening by paying full attention to your team members when they speak, asking thoughtful questions, and acknowledging their concerns.
- Show Genuine Interest: Take the time to learn about your team members' personal interests, hobbies, and backgrounds. Showing genuine interest in them as individuals helps build rapport and trust.

14.2.2 Leading by Example

As a leader, your behavior sets the tone for the rest of the team. By leading by example, you demonstrate the values and work ethic that you expect from others. Leading by example builds trust and credibility because your team can see that you practice what you preach.

How to Lead by Example:

- Demonstrate Integrity: Be honest, transparent, and ethical in your actions. If you make a mistake, own up to it and work to correct it. Your team will respect you more for your honesty.
- Work Hard and Stay Focused: Show your commitment to the team's success by working hard and staying focused on the team's goals. Your team is more likely to follow suit when they see you putting in the effort.
- Model Positive Behavior: Model the behaviors you want to see in your team, whether it's punctuality, collaboration, or open communication. Consistently displaying these behaviors encourages your team to do the same.

14.2.3 Encouraging Open Communication

Open and honest communication is essential for building trust within a team. Encourage your team members to share their ideas, concerns, and feedback freely. Creating an environment where team members feel comfortable speaking up fosters collaboration and helps address issues before they escalate.

How to Foster Open Communication:
- Create a Safe Space for Feedback: Let your team know that their feedback is valued and that they can speak openly without fear of retribution. Be receptive to both positive and constructive feedback.
- Communicate Regularly: Hold regular team meetings and one-on-one check-ins to keep the lines of communication open. Use these meetings to provide updates, discuss challenges, and gather input from the team.
- Be Transparent: Keep your team informed about organizational changes, goals, and decisions that affect their work. Transparency helps build trust and ensures that everyone is on the same page.

14.3 Establishing Your Leadership Style

Every leader has a unique leadership style, and part of your success as a new leader depends on finding a style that works for you and your team. Whether you prefer a more hands-on approach or a more hands-off style, your leadership should adapt to the needs of your team and the demands of the situation.

14.3.1 Identifying Your Leadership Style

There are several common leadership styles, each with its own strengths and challenges. Understanding your natural tendencies can help you tailor your leadership approach to different situations.

Common Leadership Styles:
- Democratic Leadership: Involves seeking input and feedback from team members before making decisions. This style fosters collaboration and ensures that everyone feels heard.
- Transformational Leadership: Focuses on inspiring and motivating team members to achieve their full potential. Transformational leaders set a vision and encourage innovation.
- Transactional Leadership: Based on a clear structure of rewards and penalties. This style is often effective in environments where tasks are well-defined and consistency is key.
- Servant Leadership: Prioritizes the needs of the team above all else. Servant leaders focus on empowering and developing their team members, often taking a supportive, behind-the-scenes role.
- Autocratic Leadership: Involves making decisions unilaterally and maintaining control over the team's actions. This style can be effective in high-pressure situations where quick decisions are needed but may limit creativity.

Pro Tip: Effective leaders often adapt their style to the needs of their team and the specific situation. While you may have a preferred style, remain flexible and open to adjusting your approach based on the context.

14.3.2 Balancing Authority and Empowerment

As a leader, you'll need to strike a balance between providing guidance and giving your team the autonomy to make decisions and take ownership of their work. Micromanaging can stifle creativity and morale, while being too hands-off may leave the team feeling unsupported.

How to Balance Authority and Empowerment:
- Set Clear Expectations: Clearly communicate the team's goals, priorities, and desired outcomes. Ensure that each team member understands their role and what is expected of them.
- Delegate Effectively: Trust your team members to handle tasks and projects on their own. Delegate responsibilities based on their strengths and skills, and provide the resources they need to succeed.
- Provide Guidance When Needed: While it's important to give your team autonomy, be available to provide guidance or support when they face challenges. Encourage them to come to you with questions or concerns.

14.3.3 Navigating Challenges as a New Leader

Transitioning into a leadership role comes with its own set of challenges. Whether you're facing resistance from team members or struggling to manage your time effectively, it's important to approach challenges with patience and a problem-solving mindset.

Common Leadership Challenges:
- Gaining Buy-In from the Team: As a new leader, you may encounter resistance from team members who are uncertain about your leadership style or vision. To gain their trust, demonstrate your commitment to their success and actively seek their input.
- Balancing Leadership with Other Responsibilities: As a leader, you'll need to manage your time effectively to balance leadership responsibilities with your own workload. Use time management strategies, such as prioritizing tasks and delegating where appropriate, to stay organized.
- Handling Difficult Conversations: Leaders are often required to have difficult conversations, whether it's providing critical feedback or addressing conflicts. Approach these conversations with empathy and transparency, focusing on finding solutions rather than assigning blame.

Chapter 15: Transitioning from Military to Civilian Life: A Guide for Service Members

For military service members, transitioning to civilian life is a significant life event that brings both opportunities and challenges. After years of service, returning to civilian life involves adjusting to new routines, finding meaningful employment, and navigating a vastly different work culture. While the transition can be daunting, careful planning, leveraging military skills, and utilizing available resources can make the shift smoother and set you up for long-term success.

This chapter will focus on helping military service members successfully transition to civilian life, with emphasis on career planning, leveraging military experience, navigating the civilian job market, and accessing available support networks.

15.1 Understanding the Challenges of Transitioning to Civilian Life

Transitioning from military to civilian life involves more than just finding a new job—it requires adapting to a new way of living, working, and thinking. Recognizing the challenges that come with this transition is the first step toward overcoming them.

15.1.1 Common Challenges for Service Members

Many service members face similar challenges during the transition, including:

- Identity Shift: After years of identifying as a service member, it can be difficult to redefine yourself as a civilian. You may feel a loss of purpose or struggle to adjust to a less structured lifestyle.
- Cultural Differences: Civilian workplaces often have different norms, communication styles, and expectations compared to the military. Adjusting to a more relaxed hierarchy or different leadership styles can be challenging.
- Translating Military Skills: Service members often struggle to articulate their military experience in a way that resonates with civilian employers. It can be difficult to translate military jargon into civilian language.
- Employment Opportunities: While military experience is highly valuable, finding a civilian job that matches your skills and interests may take time. Understanding the civilian job market and knowing how to present yourself to employers is crucial.

15.1.2 Preparing Mentally for the Transition

Transitioning from military service to civilian life requires mental preparation. Understanding that this shift is not just about finding a new career, but about adjusting to a new lifestyle, will help you approach it with the right mindset.

Mental Preparation Strategies:
- Be Patient: The transition can take time. Be patient with yourself and recognize that adjusting to civilian life is a process.
- Set Realistic Expectations: Not everything will fall into place immediately. Set realistic goals for your transition and break them into smaller, manageable steps.
- Acknowledge the Emotional Impact: You may experience a range of emotions during your transition, from excitement to anxiety. It's normal to feel uncertain, and reaching out for support is key.

15.2 Leveraging Your Military Experience in Civilian Life

One of the most valuable assets you bring to the civilian workforce is your military experience. The leadership, discipline, problem-solving skills, and work ethic you developed in the military are highly sought after by employers. The challenge is learning how to present these skills in a way that civilian employers can understand.

15.2.1 Translating Military Skills for Civilian Employers

Many military skills are transferable to civilian jobs, but you need to know how to communicate them in civilian terms. When applying for jobs or writing your resume, avoid using military jargon and instead focus on the core skills you developed.

Examples of Translatable Skills:
- Leadership: As a military leader, you likely managed teams, developed strategic plans, and made high-stakes decisions. Highlight your ability to lead teams, manage operations, and drive results.
- Discipline and Work Ethic: Employers value employees who are reliable, self-motivated, and disciplined. Your military experience shows that you can follow through on tasks, meet deadlines, and maintain a high level of professionalism.
- Problem-Solving Under Pressure: In the military, you've likely solved complex problems in high-stress environments. This ability to think critically, adapt, and remain calm under pressure is highly valuable in many industries.
- Teamwork and Collaboration: The military requires a high level of collaboration, and this teamwork experience can be a major asset in civilian jobs where working with diverse teams is critical to success.

Pro Tip: Use civilian-friendly terms on your resume and in interviews. For example, instead of saying "platoon leader," you could say "team manager responsible for overseeing operations and personnel."

15.2.2 Highlighting Your Soft Skills

In addition to technical skills, your military service has likely equipped you with essential soft skills, such as communication, adaptability, and leadership. These skills are often harder to quantify but are crucial to success in civilian roles.

Key Soft Skills to Highlight:
- Adaptability: Military service requires flexibility and the ability to adapt to new environments. Highlight your ability to thrive in dynamic, fast-paced settings.
- Leadership: Whether you led small teams or large units, your leadership experience in the military demonstrates your ability to manage people and projects.
- Communication: The ability to communicate effectively — whether giving orders, briefing senior officers, or collaborating with different departments — is highly valued in civilian roles.

15.3 Navigating the Civilian Job Market

Finding a job in the civilian workforce is one of the most critical aspects of your transition. The civilian job market operates differently from the military, and understanding how to approach it can significantly improve your chances of success.

15.3.1 Crafting a Civilian-Friendly Resume

Your resume is your first opportunity to make a strong impression on civilian employers. Tailor your resume to highlight relevant skills, experiences, and accomplishments that align with the job you're applying for.

Tips for Crafting a Civilian Resume:
- Focus on Accomplishments: Use bullet points to list your key achievements, focusing on measurable results (e.g., "Reduced operational costs by 15% through process improvements").
- Use Civilian Job Titles: When listing your military positions, translate your job titles into civilian equivalents. For example, instead of "Squad Leader," you might say "Team Supervisor."
- Highlight Relevant Skills: Tailor your resume to each job by emphasizing the skills and experiences that are most relevant to the position you're applying for.

15.3.2 Searching for Civilian Jobs

There are numerous resources available to help service members find civilian employment. Knowing where to search for jobs and how to connect with potential employers is essential.

Job Search Strategies:
- Veteran-Specific Job Boards: Websites such as Hire Heroes USA, Military.com, and VetJobs are specifically designed to help veterans find employment. These platforms often have job postings from companies that are actively seeking veterans.
- Networking: Leverage your military network and connect with veterans who have successfully transitioned to civilian careers. Networking can help you learn about job opportunities and get valuable advice.

- LinkedIn: Build a strong LinkedIn profile and connect with professionals in industries that interest you. Many recruiters actively search for veteran talent on LinkedIn, so ensure your profile reflects your skills and experience.

15.3.3 Interview Preparation for Veterans

Interviews in the civilian workforce are often different from military evaluations. Civilian interviews typically focus on behavioral questions, where you're asked to provide examples of past experiences to demonstrate your skills and qualifications.

How to Prepare for Civilian Interviews:
- Practice Common Interview Questions: Be prepared to answer common interview questions such as, "Tell me about a time you led a team" or "Describe how you handled a difficult situation." Use the STAR method (Situation, Task, Action, Result) to structure your responses.
- Discuss Your Transition: Employers may ask about your transition from the military. Be ready to explain how your military experience has prepared you for the civilian role and how your skills will benefit the organization.
- Be Confident, but Humble: Confidence is important, but avoid coming across as too rigid or overly authoritative. Civilian workplaces often value collaboration and flexibility, so show that you can work well with others in a non-hierarchical environment.

15.4 Utilizing Transition Resources

Fortunately, many organizations and government programs are dedicated to helping service members transition to civilian life. Utilizing these resources can provide you with valuable tools, connections, and support.

15.4.1 TAP (Transition Assistance Program)

The Department of Defense's Transition Assistance Program (TAP) is designed to help service members transition to civilian life. TAP offers a variety of workshops, resources, and counseling to prepare you for the civilian workforce.

Key Features of TAP:
- Employment Workshops: Learn about resume writing, job search strategies, and interview techniques through TAP's employment workshops.
- Financial Counseling: Receive guidance on managing your finances, budgeting for civilian life, and planning for retirement.
- Veteran Benefits: TAP also helps you understand the benefits available to you as a veteran, including healthcare, education, and disability benefits.

15.4.2 Veteran Service Organizations (VSOs)

Veteran Service Organizations (VSOs) provide additional resources and support for service members transitioning to civilian life. These organizations can help with everything from career counseling to legal assistance.

Examples of VSOs:
- The American Legion: Offers career fairs, employment resources, and assistance with veteran benefits.
- Veterans of Foreign Wars (VFW): Provides job training, resume assistance, and financial support for veterans.
- Disabled American Veterans (DAV): Offers career services, including job search tools and mentorship for veterans with disabilities.

15.4.3 Education and Training Benefits

For service members interested in furthering their education or acquiring new skills, the GI Bill and other educational benefits offer opportunities to pursue degrees, certifications, and vocational training.

Key Education Benefits

Post-9/11 GI Bill: The Post-9/11 GI Bill provides financial support for education and housing to eligible veterans pursuing higher education or vocational training. This benefit covers tuition, housing allowances, and books, making it a valuable resource for those looking to enhance their skills or transition into a new career field.

Veteran Readiness and Employment (VR&E): Also known as Chapter 31, this program is available to veterans with service-connected disabilities and helps them prepare for, find, and maintain suitable employment. It can include tuition assistance, job placement services, and counseling.

SkillBridge Program: The Department of Defense SkillBridge Program offers transitioning service members the opportunity to gain civilian work experience through internships, apprenticeships, and training programs during the last 180 days of service. This program can provide valuable hands-on experience and help you secure a civilian job before leaving the military.

15.5 Setting Goals for a Successful Transition

A key component of a smooth transition is setting clear, achievable goals that guide your journey from military to civilian life. These goals should cover both your professional aspirations and your personal well-being, helping you create a balanced and fulfilling life post-service.

15.5.1 Career Goals

The cornerstone of your transition will likely be your career goals. What do you want to achieve in your civilian career? Whether it's advancing in a specific industry, starting your own business, or gaining new certifications, setting clear career goals is essential.

How to Set Career Goals:
- Short-Term Goals: These might include finding a job within a certain timeframe, completing a certification program, or expanding your professional network. For example, "Obtain a project management certification within six months."
- Long-Term Goals: Think about where you want to be in your career in the next five or ten years. This could involve advancing to a leadership position or transitioning into a completely new field. For example, "Secure a managerial position in logistics within five years."

15.5.2 Personal and Financial Goals

Transitioning out of the military also affects your personal and financial life. Set goals that support your long-term well-being and stability.

Examples of Personal and Financial Goals:
- Personal: This might include building a daily routine, spending more time with family, or engaging in hobbies that improve your quality of life.
- Financial: If you're receiving retirement benefits, make sure to integrate those into your long-term financial planning. Consider setting goals like paying off debt, saving for a house, or building an emergency fund. Tools like financial counseling through TAP can help you create a sustainable financial plan.

15.5.3 Health and Well-Being Goals

Maintaining both your physical and mental health is critical during this period of transition. The military provided a structured environment, and transitioning to a less regimented civilian lifestyle can impact your well-being. Setting health and wellness goals will help you stay grounded.

Health and Well-Being Tips:
- Stay Active: Regular exercise can improve both your physical health and mental resilience. Whether it's continuing your fitness routine or trying new activities, keeping active can help ease the transition.
- Seek Mental Health Support if Needed: Transitioning can be stressful, and it's important to address any mental health concerns early on. The VA offers mental health services for veterans, and there are many organizations like Give an Hour or The Wounded Warrior Project that provide counseling and support.

15.6 Long-Term Success: Thriving in Civilian Life

Successfully transitioning to civilian life is about more than just finding a job. It's about building a sustainable, fulfilling life outside of the military while maintaining the skills, discipline, and values that shaped your service. By setting both professional and personal goals, leveraging available resources, and maintaining a focus on growth, you can create a strong foundation for long-term success.

15.6.1 Finding Purpose and Fulfillment

For many service members, a key challenge is finding purpose in civilian life after leaving the military. Your military service was likely driven by a strong sense of mission, and finding a similar sense of purpose in civilian life can be essential for long-term satisfaction.

How to Find Purpose After the Military:
- Engage in Meaningful Work: Look for a civilian career that aligns with your values and gives you a sense of accomplishment. Many veterans find fulfillment in careers related to service, such as law enforcement, healthcare, education, or nonprofit work.
- Volunteer or Give Back: Many veterans find purpose through volunteering or getting involved in their communities. Organizations like Team Rubicon allow veterans to use their skills in disaster response, providing both a sense of purpose and camaraderie.
- Pursue Education or Personal Growth: Furthering your education or developing new skills can provide a sense of purpose and progress. Use the GI Bill or other educational benefits to pursue passions that can lead to long-term fulfillment.

15.6.2 Staying Connected to the Veteran Community

Even after transitioning to civilian life, maintaining connections with the veteran community can provide a source of support, camaraderie, and shared experiences. Staying involved in veteran organizations can help you navigate post-military life with the backing of a supportive network.

Ways to Stay Connected:
- Join Veteran Networks: Organizations like the Veteran Business Network, Iraq and Afghanistan Veterans of America (IAVA), and Student Veterans of America (SVA) can help you stay connected and provide resources for career advancement and personal growth.
- Attend Veteran Events: Many cities and organizations host events for veterans, such as job fairs, networking mixers, and social gatherings. These events provide opportunities to meet fellow veterans, build relationships, and learn about resources.
- Mentor Other Veterans: Once you've successfully transitioned to civilian life, consider giving back by mentoring other service members who are going through

the process. Mentorship helps reinforce your sense of purpose and allows you to share the lessons you've learned.

Conclusion

Transitioning from military service to civilian life is a significant change, but with proper planning, a strong support network, and a focus on leveraging your military skills, you can thrive in your new career and life. Take advantage of the many resources available to veterans, set clear personal and professional goals, and remain flexible as you navigate this new chapter.

Your military service has equipped you with valuable skills, resilience, and leadership abilities that can lead to a successful and fulfilling civilian life. By approaching the transition thoughtfully and strategically, you can find purpose, build a rewarding career, and create a life that reflects the values you've developed throughout your military service.

Chapter 16: Navigating Career and Life as a Military Spouse Overseas

Military spouses play an essential role in supporting their families and service members, and for those living overseas, the challenges can be even more complex. While living in another country can offer incredible experiences, it often comes with difficulties, especially when it comes to building a career, accessing resources, and navigating a foreign culture. For military spouses stationed abroad, balancing personal goals with the demands of military life requires flexibility, resilience, and the ability to leverage available resources effectively.

This chapter will explore strategies for military spouses to build successful careers while living overseas, adapt to life in a new culture, and maintain a sense of purpose and personal well-being during their time abroad.

16.1 Understanding the Unique Challenges of Life Overseas

Living overseas as a military spouse presents both opportunities and challenges. While it can be a rewarding experience to live in a different country, the realities of adjusting to a new environment, culture, and job market can create obstacles that require thoughtful planning and adaptation.

16.1.1 Common Challenges for Military Spouses Overseas

Military spouses face several unique challenges while living abroad, including:
- Limited Job Opportunities: Depending on your location, local job opportunities may be limited, especially if language barriers exist or your career requires specific certifications that are not recognized in your host country.
- Isolation and Cultural Adjustment: Living far from home, family, and friends can lead to feelings of isolation, particularly in countries where the culture, language, and customs differ significantly from those of your home country.
- Frequent Moves: The transient nature of military life can make it difficult to build a stable career or form long-lasting friendships, especially when deployments or relocations occur frequently.
- Lack of Familiar Resources: Accessing familiar resources, such as healthcare, child care, and support services, can be more difficult when overseas. Navigating foreign systems may add an additional layer of complexity to daily life.

16.1.2 Embracing the Opportunities

Despite the challenges, living overseas also offers unique opportunities that can enrich both your personal and professional life. With the right mindset and resources, you can make the most of your time abroad.

Opportunities Overseas:
- Cultural Experiences: Living in another country allows you to experience new cultures, languages, and customs firsthand, enriching your personal development and broadening your worldview.
- Travel: Being stationed overseas often opens up travel opportunities to explore new regions and countries that might otherwise be difficult to visit.
- Networking with Other Military Spouses: Overseas military communities are often close-knit, offering a chance to form strong bonds with other military families. These connections can provide emotional support and valuable resources.

16.2 Building a Portable Career

For military spouses, building a career that can move with you is essential, especially when stationed overseas. A portable career allows you to maintain professional continuity, grow your skills, and pursue personal goals, no matter where you're located.

16.2.1 Identifying Careers That Travel Well

A portable career is one that can be done remotely, freelanced, or is in demand worldwide. Many industries offer career paths that allow military spouses to work from any location or transfer their skills between countries.

Examples of Portable Careers:
- Remote Work: Many industries, including IT, marketing, writing, customer service, and project management, offer remote work opportunities. Companies increasingly allow employees to work from anywhere, making it possible to build a stable remote career while living abroad.
- Freelancing or Consulting: If you have specialized skills in areas like graphic design, writing, accounting, or consulting, freelancing can offer the flexibility needed for a career that moves with you. Platforms like Upwork, Fiverr, or Freelancer can help you find clients globally.
- Education and Teaching: Teaching, especially English as a Second Language (ESL), is a popular option for military spouses abroad. Online teaching platforms like VIPKid, Cambly, or Tutor.com allow you to teach from home, while some countries may offer in-person teaching opportunities.
- Healthcare: Some healthcare professions, such as nursing, therapy, or medical transcription, may allow for portability with the right certifications or licenses. Telehealth services also offer remote options for qualified professionals.

16.2.2 Leveraging Military Spouse Employment Programs

The military and various organizations provide employment support for military spouses, including those living overseas. These programs can help you find remote work, identify portable careers, or offer training and education to enhance your employability.

Employment Programs for Military Spouses

- Military Spouse Employment Partnership (MSEP): MSEP connects military spouses with employers who are committed to hiring them. It offers resources for finding remote work or on-base employment.

- Spouse Education and Career Opportunities (SECO): SECO provides career counseling, education, and training resources specifically designed for military spouses. It also offers access to job boards and employment workshops.

- USAJOBS - Military Spouses: The federal government offers specific job listings and hiring preferences for military spouses through the USAJOBS platform, making it easier to find federal positions both in the U.S. and abroad.

- MyCAA Scholarship Program: The My Career Advancement Account (MyCAA) program offers up to $4,000 in financial assistance for eligible military spouses to pursue education, licenses, or certifications that support portable careers.

Pro Tip: Take advantage of remote job boards like FlexJobs, We Work Remotely, and Remote.co to find flexible employment options that align with your skills and goals.

16.3 Navigating Local Job Markets and Employment Laws

Finding a job in the local economy can be more complicated when living overseas due to varying employment laws, language barriers, and credential recognition. Understanding the local job market and employment regulations is crucial for military spouses seeking work abroad.

16.3.1 Understanding SOFA and Work Authorization

In many cases, military spouses living abroad are governed by the Status of Forces Agreement (SOFA), which outlines the legal status of military personnel and their dependents in the host country. SOFA can impact your ability to work in the local economy.

Key Considerations:
- Work Authorization: Depending on the SOFA agreement between your host country and the U.S., you may need a work permit or special authorization to work off-base in the local economy. Ensure you understand the legal requirements before applying for local jobs.
- Base Employment: Some overseas military installations offer employment opportunities for spouses in areas such as childcare, education, retail, or administrative work. These jobs are often easier to secure than positions in the local economy.

16.3.2 Overcoming Language Barriers

In non-English-speaking countries, language barriers can be a significant obstacle to finding work or integrating into the local community. However, taking steps to learn the local language can open up more opportunities.

How to Overcome Language Barriers:
- Language Classes: Many military installations offer language classes to help spouses learn the local language. Additionally, platforms like Duolingo, Babbel, or local language schools can help you build language skills.
- Translation and Language Apps: Use translation tools like Google Translate to assist with communication in everyday situations. While not a substitute for fluency, these tools can help you navigate daily interactions.
- Networking with Bilingual Locals: Connect with locals who are bilingual in both the local language and English. They can provide support, help with cultural nuances, and offer advice on job opportunities.

16.4 Adapting to a New Culture and Maintaining Well-Being

Living in a foreign country can be both exciting and challenging, and adapting to a new culture is a key part of making the most of your overseas experience. Taking steps to integrate into your host country's culture while maintaining your mental and emotional well-being is crucial for a fulfilling experience.

16.4.1 Embracing Cultural Differences

Living in a different country exposes you to new customs, traditions, and social norms. Embracing these differences rather than resisting them can help you adjust more smoothly to life overseas.

Tips for Adapting to a New Culture:
- Learn About the Culture: Take time to learn about the local customs, traditions, and etiquette of your host country. Understanding the cultural context can help you avoid misunderstandings and build better relationships with locals.
- Be Open-Minded and Curious: Approach cultural differences with curiosity and openness. Try new foods, attend local events, and participate in cultural experiences that allow you to immerse yourself in the local way of life.
- Build Relationships with Locals: Make an effort to connect with locals, whether through language classes, community events, or volunteer opportunities. Building relationships with locals can enrich your experience and help you feel more at home.

16.4.2 Staying Connected with Loved Ones

Living far from home can lead to feelings of isolation, but staying connected with family and friends can provide a sense of stability and emotional support.

Ways to Stay Connected:
- Use Technology: Take advantage of video calls, messaging apps, and social media to stay in touch with loved ones back home. Regular virtual check-ins can help you feel more connected.
- Plan Visits: If possible, plan visits from family and friends or take trips home during leave periods. Having something to look forward to can ease feelings of homesickness.
- Join Local Support Networks: Many overseas military communities have spouse support groups, social clubs, or family resource centers that offer events and activities designed to help spouses connect with one another.

16.4.3 Prioritizing Self-Care and Mental Health

Maintaining your mental and physical well-being is essential, especially when navigating the challenges of living overseas. Practicing self-care and seeking support when needed can help you manage the stresses of military life abroad and maintain your overall well-being.

Self-Care Strategies for Military Spouses:
- Establish a Routine: Create a daily routine that includes activities that help you stay grounded, such as exercise, meditation, reading, or pursuing hobbies. A routine can provide structure and help you maintain a sense of control, even in an unfamiliar environment.
- Stay Physically Active: Exercise is an excellent way to reduce stress, improve mental health, and stay healthy. Join fitness classes on base, explore local outdoor activities, or follow online workout programs that you can do from home.
- Seek Support for Mental Health: If you're feeling overwhelmed, don't hesitate to seek professional help. Many military installations offer counseling services for spouses, and the Military OneSource program provides free, confidential counseling sessions by phone or online.
- Practice Mindfulness and Stress Management: Living abroad can be stressful, especially during transitions or deployments. Incorporate mindfulness practices, such as meditation or journaling, into your routine to help manage stress and maintain emotional balance.

16.5 Leveraging Available Resources for Military Spouses

The military provides numerous resources to help spouses navigate the challenges of living overseas, including employment support, educational opportunities, and mental health services. By taking advantage of these resources, you can build a fulfilling life abroad while supporting your family.

16.5.1 Military OneSource

Military OneSource is a comprehensive support service that offers a wide range of resources for military spouses, including those living overseas. It provides free, confidential counseling, financial planning assistance, relocation support, and career resources.

Key Services Offered by Military OneSource:
- Counseling Services: Spouses can access free, non-medical counseling sessions for issues such as stress, relationships, parenting, and adjustment to military life. These services are available online or by phone.
- Relocation Assistance: Military OneSource offers relocation resources, such as information on moving overseas, housing options, and settling into a new community.
- Employment and Education Support: The platform provides access to career coaching, resume assistance, job search resources, and information about educational opportunities like the MyCAA scholarship program.

16.5.2 Spouse Education and Career Opportunities (SECO)

SECO offers personalized career counseling and education resources to military spouses. Whether you're looking to start or continue a career, SECO can help you navigate the unique challenges of military life, including overseas relocations.

SECO Services Include:
- Career Coaching: Speak with a SECO career coach for personalized guidance on developing a career plan, exploring educational opportunities, or finding portable job options.
- Resume and Interview Support: SECO provides resources for building a strong resume and preparing for job interviews, both remotely and in local job markets.
- Portable Career Training: Through the SECO platform, you can find training programs and certifications that help you build a career that can move with you, such as healthcare, IT, or project management.

16.5.3 Installation-Specific Resources

Each overseas military installation typically has specific resources for military spouses, such as spouse clubs, volunteer opportunities, education centers, and employment offices. These on-base services can help you connect with other spouses, find local employment, and access educational or training opportunities.

Examples of Installation-Specific Resources:
- Army Community Services/Family Readiness Centers: These centers provide resources and programs that promote the well-being of military families. They may offer counseling services, financial education, and support during deployments.

- Military Spouse Clubs: Many installations have spouse clubs or social groups that organize events, provide mutual support, and offer networking opportunities. Joining these clubs can help you build friendships and find a sense of community.
- On-Base Employment Offices: Some installations have employment offices that assist military spouses in finding work on base, such as administrative positions, retail, or childcare.

16.6 Setting Goals for Your Overseas

Experience living overseas as a military spouse provides an opportunity for both personal and professional growth. By setting clear goals, you can make the most of your time abroad and create a fulfilling experience that aligns with your long-term aspirations.

16.6.1 Personal Growth and Learning

Consider setting goals that focus on personal development while living overseas. These goals could include learning the local language, exploring new cultures, or pursuing hobbies that you've always wanted to try.

Examples of Personal Goals:
- Learn the Local Language: Set a goal to achieve a certain level of fluency in the language spoken in your host country. This can help you feel more integrated into the local culture and increase job opportunities.
- Explore the Region: Make a list of places you'd like to visit while stationed overseas, and set travel goals for each year. Exploring nearby countries or cities can enrich your overseas experience.
- Develop New Hobbies: Use your time abroad to explore hobbies such as photography, painting, or gardening. Many military bases offer recreational activities and classes that allow you to learn something new.

16.6.2 Career Development

If maintaining or building a career is important to you, set specific goals that align with your professional aspirations. These goals could include obtaining certifications, starting a remote business, or expanding your network.

Examples of Career Goals:
- Obtain Certifications: If your career field requires certifications, set a goal to complete the necessary courses while overseas. Many online platforms, such as Coursera or edX, offer professional certifications that can be completed remotely.
- Start a Freelance Business: If freelancing is part of your career plan, set measurable goals for securing clients, building a portfolio, or increasing your income each year.
- Expand Your Network: Set a goal to connect with other professionals in your industry, both in person and online. Attend virtual industry events, join LinkedIn

groups, or participate in online forums to build relationships that can support your career.

16.6.3 Family and Community Involvement

Being overseas is also an opportunity to strengthen family bonds and get involved in the military and local communities. Set goals that promote family time, volunteer work, or involvement in spouse organizations.

Examples of Family and Community Goals:
- Strengthen Family Bonds: Set a goal to spend quality time with your family by planning activities, such as family outings, game nights, or cultural experiences in your host country.
- Volunteer Locally: Many military spouses find fulfillment through volunteering. Look for volunteer opportunities on base or in the local community that align with your interests and values.
- Get Involved in Spouse Organizations: Participate in spouse clubs or military support groups to meet other spouses, share experiences, and contribute to the military community.

Conclusion

Living overseas as a military spouse presents both challenges and opportunities. By approaching your time abroad with an open mind, a commitment to personal growth, and a focus on building a portable career, you can create a fulfilling and rewarding experience. Leverage the many resources available to military spouses, connect with other families in the military community, and set clear goals to make the most of your overseas assignment.

Chapter 17: Navigating the Federal Employment Process: A Guide for Military Service Members, Veterans, Military Spouses, and Civilians

Applying for federal employment can be a valuable career path for military service members, veterans, and military spouses. The federal government offers job security, competitive benefits, and meaningful work in a variety of fields. However, the application process for federal jobs can be complex, requiring patience, attention to detail, and an understanding of how to navigate the system effectively.

In this chapter, we'll cover the federal employment process in depth, from preparing your application to navigating the USAJOBS platform, writing effective federal resumes, and understanding the hiring preferences available to veterans and military spouses.

17.1 Understanding the Federal Hiring Process

The federal hiring process differs significantly from the private sector. Federal agencies follow strict guidelines set by the U.S. Office of Personnel Management (OPM), which govern how job announcements are posted, how applications are evaluated, and how candidates are selected.

17.1.1 Key Steps in the Federal Hiring Process

The federal hiring process typically follows these steps:
1. Job Announcement: Federal agencies post job openings on USAJOBS, the official government job board. Each job announcement includes details about the position, required qualifications, application instructions, and deadlines.
2. Application Submission: Applicants submit their application materials, usually including a federal resume, cover letter, and any other required documents (e.g., transcripts, veteran preference documents).
3. Eligibility and Qualifications Review: Human resources (HR) personnel review applications to determine if candidates meet the basic eligibility and qualification requirements based on education, experience, and skills.
4. Assessment: Candidates may be required to complete assessments such as questionnaires or tests to further evaluate their qualifications.
5. Referral List: Qualified applicants are placed on a referral list, which is sent to the hiring manager for further review.
6. Interviews: The hiring manager selects candidates for interviews based on the referral list. Some positions may require multiple rounds of interviews.
7. Selection: After the interviews, the hiring manager makes a selection, and the candidate is offered the position.
8. Background Check and Security Clearance: Once a candidate is selected, they may need to undergo a background check and obtain security clearance, depending on the job.

17.2 Creating a USAJOBS Profile

USAJOBS is the central platform for federal job listings, and creating a detailed profile on the site is the first step in applying for federal jobs. Your USAJOBS profile allows you to search for jobs, save job announcements, and submit applications.

17.2.1 Setting Up Your USAJOBS Profile

To get started on USAJOBS, you'll need to create an account and complete your profile. This information will be used to help tailor your job searches and streamline the application process.

Steps to Set Up Your Profile:
1. Create an Account: Visit the USAJOBS website (www.usajobs.gov) and create an account by providing your name, email address, and a secure password.
2. Complete the Profile: Your profile includes sections for personal information, education, employment history, and preferences. Make sure to fill out all fields as completely as possible, as this information can help you match with jobs that fit your qualifications.
3. Upload Required Documents: USAJOBS allows you to upload documents that may be required for applications, such as your resume, transcripts, veteran preference documents (DD-214), or SF-50 (Notification of Personnel Action) for current federal employees.

17.2.2 Setting Job Preferences

In your USAJOBS profile, you can set preferences for the types of jobs you're looking for, including location, work schedule (full-time, part-time), and pay grade. Tailoring these preferences can help refine your job search and alert you to relevant opportunities.

Customizing Your Job Preferences:
- Job Categories: Select the categories that match your skills and experience. For example, if you have a background in IT, choose categories like "Information Technology Management."
- Location Preferences: Indicate where you're willing to work, whether it's domestic, overseas, or specific cities.
- Pay Grade: Pay grades in the federal system are based on the General Schedule (GS) scale. Be sure to select the pay grade that matches your experience and qualifications. If you're unsure of your appropriate grade, many job announcements provide guidance.

17.3 Writing an Effective Federal Resume

A federal resume is different from a private-sector resume. It's typically longer, more detailed, and must include specific information that aligns with federal hiring standards. Writing a strong federal resume is crucial to successfully navigating the federal hiring process.

17.3.1 Key Differences Between Federal and Private-Sector Resumes

Federal resumes are generally more comprehensive than those used in the private sector.

Here are some key differences:
- Length: Federal resumes are often 4-6 pages long, compared to the 1-2 pages typically used in the private sector. This is because federal resumes require more detailed information about your work experience and qualifications.
- Detail: You must include specific details about your work history, including job duties, accomplishments, the number of hours worked per week, and salary information for each position.
- Keywords: Federal resumes must include keywords from the job announcement. These keywords reflect the qualifications and duties required for the position and are used by HR to screen applications.
- Focus on Accomplishments: Federal hiring managers want to see measurable results, so emphasize your accomplishments by providing specific examples and quantifying your impact (e.g., "Managed a team of 10 to reduce project delivery time by 15%").

17.3.2 Essential Sections for a Federal Resume

Your federal resume should include the following sections:
- Personal Information: Include your full name, contact information, citizenship status, and whether you've worked for the federal government before.
- Objective or Summary: A brief statement summarizing your qualifications, career goals, and how you align with the position.
- Work Experience: Provide detailed descriptions of each position, including job title, agency or company name, location, dates of employment, number of hours worked per week, salary, and supervisor's contact information (or indicate if the supervisor can't be contacted).
- Education: List all relevant education, including degrees, certifications, and any relevant training. Include the school's name, degree or certification received, graduation date, and GPA (if required).
- Skills: Highlight technical and soft skills that align with the job. Include relevant computer programs, software, and industry-specific skills.
- Certifications and Awards: Include any certifications, licenses, awards, or honors you've received that are relevant to the job.

17.3.3 Using the USAJOBS Resume Builder

USAJOBS offers a built-in resume builder, which can be helpful for ensuring that your resume meets the necessary federal standards. The resume builder guides you through each section and prompts you to include all required information.

Benefits of Using the USAJOBS Resume Builder:
- Ensures Compliance: By using the resume builder, you can ensure that your resume includes all required details, such as employment dates, hours worked per week, and salary information.
- Simplifies Updates: You can save multiple versions of your resume and update them easily as you apply for different jobs.
- Integrated with Job Applications: The resume builder automatically formats your resume for submission through the USAJOBS platform, ensuring compatibility with the system.

17.4 Understanding Veterans' Preference and Military Spouse Hiring Preferences

The federal government is committed to hiring veterans and military spouses, offering specific hiring preferences and programs that make it easier for these groups to secure federal jobs.

17.4.1 Veterans' Preference

Veterans' preference gives eligible veterans priority in federal hiring. This preference applies to competitive service positions and can significantly improve your chances of being selected for a job.

Types of Veterans' Preference:
- 5-Point Preference: Veterans who served during specific periods of war or received a campaign badge can receive 5 points added to their application score.
- 10-Point Preference: Veterans with a service-connected disability, Purple Heart recipients, and certain other groups are eligible for 10 points of preference.

How to Apply for Veterans' Preference:
- Submit Documentation: When applying for federal jobs, submit your DD-214 (Certificate of Release or Discharge from Active Duty) and any disability documentation (if applicable) to claim veterans' preference.
- Understand Special Hiring Authorities: Veterans may also be eligible for special hiring authorities, such as the Veterans Recruitment Appointment (VRA), which allows agencies to hire eligible veterans non-competitively.

17.4.2 Military Spouse Preference

Military spouses may qualify for a non-competitive hiring process through the Military Spouse Non-Competitive Appointment Authority, which allows federal agencies to appoint military spouses without going through the competitive hiring process.

Eligibility for Military Spouse Preference:
- PCS Orders: Military spouses who are relocating due to a Permanent Change of Station (PCS) are eligible for non-competitive appointments.
- Disability or Death of a Service Member: Spouses of service members who were disabled or died in active duty may also be eligible.

How to Apply for Military Spouse Preference:
- Submit Documentation: When applying, submit supporting documentation, such as your spouse's PCS orders or proof of disability/death if applicable.
- Search for Jobs on USAJOBS: Many federal positions specify that military spouses are eligible for preference, and USAJOBS allows you to filter searches to show jobs for which you qualify.

17.5 Preparing for the Interview and Beyond

Once your application has been reviewed and you've been referred for an interview, it's time to prepare for this next crucial step in the federal hiring process. Interviews for federal positions may be different from those in the private sector, and they require a thorough understanding of the agency's mission, as well as how your experience aligns with the role.

17.5.1 Understanding the Federal Interview Process

Federal job interviews are often more structured than private-sector interviews. Interviewers typically ask a standardized set of questions, which allows them to fairly assess each candidate against the qualifications for the position. You may encounter behavior-based or scenario-based questions that ask how you handled certain situations in the past, using the STAR method (Situation, Task, Action, Result).

Common Types of Federal Interview Questions

- Behavioral Questions: These questions ask how you've handled situations in your previous roles. For example, "Tell me about a time when you had to solve a complex problem under tight deadlines."

- Technical Questions: If you're applying for a technical role, such as in IT or engineering, expect questions that assess your technical expertise.

- Scenario-Based Questions: These questions present a hypothetical situation, and you're asked how you would handle it. For example, "How would you prioritize multiple projects with competing deadlines?"

17.5.2 Preparing for the Interview

Preparation is key to a successful interview. Thoroughly research the agency and the specific role you're applying for, practice your answers to common interview questions, and be ready to discuss how your experience and skills align with the job's requirements.

Tips for Preparing:
- Research the Agency: Understand the agency's mission, values, and priorities. Be ready to discuss how your skills and experience align with the agency's goals and how you can contribute to its success.
- Practice Using the STAR Method: For behavior-based questions, use the STAR method (Situation, Task, Action, Result) to structure your responses. Provide clear, specific examples of how you've handled similar challenges in the past.
- Prepare Questions for the Interviewer: At the end of the interview, you'll likely have the opportunity to ask questions. Prepare thoughtful questions that demonstrate your interest in the role and the agency, such as "What are the agency's current priorities, and how does this role contribute to them?"

17.5.3 Handling Multiple Interviews

It's not uncommon for federal jobs to require multiple rounds of interviews. In some cases, the first interview may be a phone or video interview, followed by in-person interviews with multiple hiring managers or panels. Treat each interview with the same level of preparation, and be ready to build upon your previous responses if asked similar questions.

17.6 Navigating Background Checks and Security Clearances

After you've been selected for a federal position, the final steps of the hiring process typically involve background checks and, for certain positions, obtaining a security clearance. This can be a lengthy process, but it's necessary to ensure that federal employees meet the necessary security and trustworthiness standards.

17.6.1 Understanding Federal Background Checks

All federal jobs require some level of background check. The level of the background check will vary depending on the job's sensitivity, and it may include verifying your employment history, criminal record, financial stability, and education.

Types of Background Checks:
- Public Trust Positions: Jobs that involve sensitive but unclassified information may require a Public Trust background check. This generally includes a review of your financial history, employment history, and criminal record.
- National Security Positions: Positions requiring access to classified information (such as intelligence, defense, or law enforcement jobs) will require a more in-depth background check and security clearance.

17.6.2 Obtaining a Security Clearance

Some federal positions require a security clearance, which is a status granted after a thorough background investigation. Clearances can range from Confidential (the lowest level) to Top Secret (the highest level). The process for obtaining a clearance involves a detailed investigation into your personal, financial, and professional history.

Levels of Security Clearances:
- Confidential: The lowest level of security clearance, typically for positions involving access to information that could damage national security if disclosed.
- Secret: A higher level of clearance for positions with access to information that could cause serious damage to national security.
- Top Secret: The highest level of clearance, required for positions with access to highly sensitive information that could cause grave damage to national security.

The Clearance Process:
- Submit an SF-86: The first step in the clearance process is completing the Standard Form 86 (SF-86), which requires detailed personal, financial, and employment information. It's critical to be thorough and truthful when completing this form.
- Investigation: After submitting the SF-86, an investigator will review your background. This may involve interviews with people who know you, as well as a review of your financial, legal, and employment records.

- Polygraph: Certain positions, especially in intelligence agencies, may require a polygraph examination as part of the clearance process.

Pro Tip: Security clearance processing times can vary widely, depending on the agency and the level of clearance required. Plan accordingly, as some clearances can take several months to process.

17.7 Navigating Special Hiring Programs for Veterans and Military Spouses

The federal government offers several special hiring programs designed to make it easier for veterans, military spouses, and transitioning service members to find federal employment.

17.7.1 Veterans Recruitment Appointment (VRA)

The VRA program allows agencies to appoint eligible veterans to positions without going through the competitive hiring process. VRA-eligible veterans can be appointed to positions at the GS-11 level or below.

Eligibility for VRA:
- Veterans with a service-connected disability.
- Veterans who served during a war or in a campaign for which a campaign badge has been authorized.
- Veterans separated within the last three years under honorable conditions.

17.7.2 Veterans Employment Opportunities Act (VEOA)

The VEOA gives veterans the opportunity to compete for federal jobs under merit promotion procedures, which are typically reserved for current federal employees. This means eligible veterans can apply for certain jobs that are not open to the general public.

17.7.3 Schedule A Hiring Authority for Individuals with Disabilities

Veterans with disabilities may be eligible for the Schedule A hiring authority, which allows federal agencies to hire individuals with disabilities without going through the competitive hiring process.

17.7.4 Non-Competitive Hiring for Military Spouses

Military spouses relocating due to a Permanent Change of Station (PCS) or those whose service member spouse is disabled or has died in service may qualify for non-competitive hiring. This can significantly streamline the federal hiring process for military spouses.

Conclusion

The federal employment process can be complex, but it offers rewarding and stable career opportunities for veterans, military spouses, and transitioning service members. By understanding the steps involved — from creating a strong USAJOBS profile to crafting a detailed federal resume, preparing for interviews, and leveraging veterans' and military spouse hiring preferences — you can navigate the system successfully.

Chapter 18: Salary Negotiation in Federal Employment: Maximizing Your Compensation

Navigating salary negotiations in the federal employment system is different from negotiating in the private sector. Federal jobs follow structured pay scales and systems that determine salary ranges based on various factors, including your experience, education, and the specific position. While the federal government has set guidelines for pay, there are still opportunities to negotiate and maximize your compensation, especially if you understand the process and know how to advocate for yourself effectively.

In this chapter, we'll explore the General Schedule (GS) pay scale, how to assess your salary level, the factors that influence pay in the federal system, and strategies for negotiating your salary during the federal hiring process.

18.1 Understanding the Federal Pay System

The federal government uses a structured pay system to determine employee salaries. The most common system is the General Schedule (GS) pay scale, which covers the majority of civilian federal jobs. However, there are other pay scales for specific roles, such as the Federal Wage System (FWS) for blue-collar workers and the Senior Executive Service (SES) for senior-level employees.

18.1.1 The General Schedule (GS) Pay Scale

The GS pay scale is divided into 15 grades (GS-1 to GS-15), with each grade having 10 steps. Your GS grade is based on the position you're hired for, and your step is determined by your experience, education, and length of service. As you gain more experience or additional qualifications, you can move up in steps or even advance to a higher GS grade.

Key Components of the GS Pay Scale:
- Grade: The GS grade reflects the difficulty, responsibility, and qualifications required for the job. Entry-level positions typically start at GS-1 or GS-2, while positions requiring more specialized experience or advanced education may start at higher grades, such as GS-7 or GS-11.
- Step: Each GS grade has 10 steps that represent pay increases within the grade. You can move to higher steps within your grade over time through satisfactory job performance or by negotiating your step level during the hiring process.
- Locality Pay: Federal employees' salaries are adjusted based on their geographic location to account for differences in the cost of living. Locality pay ensures that employees in high-cost areas (e.g., Washington, D.C., San Francisco) receive higher compensation than those in lower-cost areas.

Pro Tip: You can find the current GS pay scale and locality pay tables on the U.S. Office of Personnel Management (OPM) website. This tool can help you understand the pay range for positions in different locations.

18.1.2 Other Federal Pay Systems

In addition to the GS system, other federal pay systems are used for specific types of jobs:
- Federal Wage System (FWS): Covers blue-collar workers such as tradespeople, craftspeople, and maintenance staff. FWS pay is based on local prevailing wages and is typically lower than GS pay for similar positions.
- Senior Executive Service (SES): SES positions are reserved for senior-level executives and managers in the federal government. SES employees have more flexibility in their salaries, which are negotiated and based on experience, performance, and agency needs.
- Pay Bands: Some agencies use pay bands instead of the GS scale. Pay bands group several GS grades into broader categories and offer more flexibility in salary ranges and promotions.

18.2 Assessing Your Salary Level

Before you can negotiate your salary effectively, it's essential to understand the salary range for the position you're applying for and how your qualifications fit into that range. This involves researching the GS grade for your position, understanding the steps within that grade, and factoring in locality pay.

18.2.1 Determining Your GS Grade

The job announcement on USAJOBS will specify the GS grade or pay band for the position. Make sure you meet the qualifications for the grade listed, as this will determine your starting salary. If you're overqualified for the listed grade, you may be able to negotiate for a higher grade if the job allows for a range of grades (e.g., GS-7/9/11).

How to Determine the Appropriate GS Grade:
- Review the Qualifications: The job announcement will include a section outlining the qualifications for each grade level. If you meet or exceed the qualifications for a higher grade, you may be eligible to apply for that grade.
- Consider Your Experience and Education: Compare your experience, education, and skill set to the qualifications required for the job. Higher grades typically require more specialized experience or advanced education.

18.2.2 Understanding Steps and Locality Pay

Once you've identified the GS grade for your position, it's time to assess where you fall within the 10 steps. Starting steps are typically negotiable based on your prior experience, education, and the value you bring to the role.

Factors That Influence Your Step:
- Prior Experience: If you have relevant work experience that exceeds the minimum qualifications for the grade, you can negotiate for a higher step.
- Education: Advanced degrees or certifications that are directly related to the position may qualify you for a higher step.
- Locality Pay: Be sure to check the locality pay for the area where the job is located. This can have a significant impact on your final salary, especially in high-cost areas.

18.3 Strategies for Negotiating Your Salary

While the federal pay scale may seem rigid, there are still opportunities to negotiate your starting salary and other benefits. The key is to come prepared with a clear understanding of how your experience aligns with the position and to make a compelling case for why you deserve a higher step or salary.

18.3.1 Negotiating Your Step

If you feel that your qualifications merit a higher starting salary within your grade, you can negotiate for a higher step. This is typically done after you receive a tentative job offer, but before you formally accept the position.

How to Negotiate Your Step:
- Highlight Your Experience: Emphasize any specialized experience or skills that exceed the minimum requirements for the job. For example, if you have years of relevant experience beyond what's required for a GS-9, make the case that you should start at a higher step within that grade.
- Leverage Previous Salary: If you were earning a higher salary in a previous job, you can use that as a basis for negotiating a higher step in the federal system. Keep in mind that federal agencies may ask for documentation of your previous salary, so be prepared to provide pay stubs or other verification.
- Use Salary Research: Research the average salary for similar positions in your geographic area or industry. This can help you justify your request for a higher step.

Example Negotiation Script: "Based on my 10 years of experience in project management, which exceeds the minimum qualifications for this GS-11 position, and my previous salary at my last job, I believe that starting at Step 7 would be appropriate. This would reflect the level of expertise I bring to the role and ensure a competitive salary based on my qualifications."

18.3.2 Negotiating Relocation and Recruitment Incentives

In addition to salary, you may be able to negotiate other forms of compensation, such as relocation expenses, recruitment incentives, or signing bonuses.

Other Compensation Elements to Consider:
- Relocation Expenses: If the job requires you to move, you can negotiate for the agency to cover your relocation expenses. Some federal positions offer relocation incentives to help offset the cost of moving to a new location.
- Recruitment Incentives: In some cases, agencies may offer recruitment incentives for hard-to-fill positions. This could include a one-time signing bonus or a higher starting salary.
- Student Loan Repayment: Some federal agencies offer student loan repayment programs as an additional benefit. If you have significant student loan debt, inquire about whether this program is available.

18.4 Other Benefits to Consider

While salary is an essential component of your federal job offer, the total compensation package includes several other benefits that can add significant value. These benefits may not be negotiable, but understanding them can help you make an informed decision about your offer.

18.4.1 Retirement and Health Benefits

Federal employees have access to comprehensive retirement and health benefits, which can provide long-term financial security.

Federal Employee Benefits:
- Federal Employees Retirement System (FERS): FERS provides a retirement plan for federal employees, which includes a pension, Social Security benefits, and the Thrift Savings Plan (TSP), a defined contribution plan similar to a 401(k).
- Health Insurance: Federal employees are eligible for health insurance through the Federal Employees Health Benefits (FEHB) program, which offers a wide range of plans to choose from.
- Life Insurance: The Federal Employees' Group Life Insurance (FEGLI) program provides basic life insurance coverage, with options to increase coverage based on your needs.

18.4.2 Paid Leave and Work-Life Balance

The federal government offers generous paid leave policies and work-life balance options, which can enhance your overall compensation package.

Paid Leave and Flexibility:
- Annual Leave: Federal employees accrue annual leave based on their length of service. New employees typically start with 13 days of annual leave per year, with increases over time.
- Sick Leave: Federal employees accrue 13 days of sick leave per year, which can be used for personal illness or to care for a family member.

- Flexible Work Schedules: Many federal agencies offer flexible work schedules, telework options, and compressed workweeks to support work-life balance.

Conclusion

While the federal pay scale provides a structured system for compensation, there are still opportunities to negotiate your starting salary, step level, and other benefits when applying for federal employment. Understanding the nuances of the General Schedule (GS) pay system, researching locality pay, and highlighting your unique qualifications will strengthen your ability to secure a competitive compensation package. Additionally, considering the full range of federal benefits—including retirement plans, health insurance, and paid leave—will help you evaluate the overall value of your offer and ensure long-term financial stability.

By approaching salary negotiations with clear knowledge of the federal pay structure and your eligibility for benefits like veterans' preference or military spouse non-competitive appointments, you can advocate for a compensation package that reflects your experience and expertise. Even in cases where salary might seem fixed, negotiating for a higher step or additional incentives like relocation assistance can provide added value.

Chapter 19: Applying for Federal Employment Overseas: Opportunities and Strategies for Military Service Members, Veterans, Military Spouses, and Civilians

Federal employment overseas offers the opportunity to work in various roles within U.S. government agencies while living in another country. Whether you're a civilian exploring new career prospects, a military spouse accompanying your partner, a transitioning service member, or a veteran, overseas federal jobs provide stability, competitive benefits, and exposure to new cultural experiences. However, the application process for federal jobs abroad presents unique challenges, including understanding overseas pay structures, managing international relocation, and dealing with work authorization rules in foreign countries.

This chapter will explore how to navigate the federal hiring process for overseas positions, the compensation and benefits specific to these jobs, and strategies for successfully transitioning to life and work abroad.

19.1 Understanding Overseas Federal Employment

Federal employment overseas covers a wide range of job opportunities in U.S. embassies, military bases, consulates, and other government installations. While many of these roles are based in the Department of Defense (DoD) and the Department of State, there are opportunities across various federal agencies.

19.1.1 Types of Overseas Federal Jobs

Federal jobs overseas fall into several categories, including administrative, technical, educational, security, and diplomatic positions. Each of these categories offers distinct roles suited to various skill sets.

Common Overseas Federal Positions:
- Administrative Roles: Positions such as program assistants, administrative officers, or human resources personnel who support the operations of federal offices or military installations.
- IT and Technical Roles: IT specialists, telecommunications experts, or cybersecurity professionals working in embassy or military base infrastructure.
- Education and Childcare: Positions at Department of Defense Education Activity (DoDEA) schools or on-base childcare centers for military families.
- Security and Law Enforcement: Roles in security, such as federal protective officers or diplomatic security personnel.
- Diplomatic and Consular Positions: Opportunities to work with the State Department in roles such as foreign service officers, consular staff, or embassy support.

19.1.2 Locations and Agencies Offering Overseas Jobs

Federal employees can find overseas employment in U.S. embassies, consulates, and military bases in regions including Europe, Asia, the Middle East, and Africa. The Department of State, the Department of Defense (DoD), and other federal agencies all have overseas offices or operations that require support.

Agencies with Overseas Positions:
- Department of Defense (DoD): The largest employer of federal employees overseas, the DoD operates on U.S. military installations across the globe.
- Department of State: The U.S. Department of State employs foreign service officers, consular staff, and administrative personnel at embassies and consulates worldwide.
- Department of Homeland Security (DHS): Overseas operations include U.S. Customs and Border Protection (CBP) officers and U.S. Immigration and Customs Enforcement (ICE) staff stationed abroad.
- Other Federal Agencies: The U.S. Agency for International Development (USAID), the Central Intelligence Agency (CIA), and other agencies also maintain overseas offices that require federal employees.

19.2 Navigating the Federal Hiring Process for Overseas Jobs

The process of applying for overseas federal jobs is similar to applying for domestic positions but with additional considerations, such as understanding the logistics of relocation and the pay and benefits specific to overseas assignments.

19.2.1 Using USAJOBS to Find Overseas Jobs

USAJOBS (www.usajobs.gov) is the primary platform for federal job listings, including overseas positions. You can search specifically for overseas opportunities by selecting "U.S. Citizens Overseas" or "Military Spouses Overseas" in the location filter.

How to Find Overseas Jobs on USAJOBS:
- Search by Location: Use the location filter on USAJOBS to search for jobs in specific countries or regions where federal positions are available. Popular regions for overseas jobs include Germany, Japan, South Korea, and Italy.
- Search by Agency: If you're targeting a specific agency, such as the Department of State or DoD, you can filter your search by agency to find relevant overseas positions.
- Use Keywords: Tailor your search by using keywords related to your field (e.g., "program management," "cybersecurity," "logistics") to find overseas jobs that match your skills.

19.2.2 Understanding Eligibility and Hiring Preferences

Federal jobs overseas often have specific eligibility requirements. Additionally, military spouses and veterans may be eligible for non-competitive hiring preferences that can improve their chances of securing a federal job overseas.

Eligibility for Overseas Federal Jobs:
- U.S. Citizenship: All federal jobs overseas require U.S. citizenship. Make sure your citizenship status is up-to-date in your USAJOBS profile.
- Security Clearance: Many overseas jobs, especially in the DoD and Department of State, require a security clearance. Be prepared to undergo the clearance process if you don't already have one.
- Special Hiring Authorities: Veterans and military spouses can take advantage of hiring authorities such as Veterans Recruitment Appointment (VRA) and Military Spouse Non-Competitive Appointment Authority, which make it easier to secure federal jobs overseas.

Pro Tip: If you're a military spouse, use the "Military Spouses" filter on USAJOBS to find positions eligible for non-competitive hiring.

19.2.3 Crafting an Overseas-Ready Federal Resume

Federal resumes for overseas jobs need to be detailed and tailored to the position and location. Since overseas positions often involve unique challenges, it's important to highlight any international experience, adaptability, and cultural awareness you bring to the table.

Tips for Crafting an Overseas Federal Resume:
- Emphasize Adaptability: Highlight your ability to adapt to new environments and work effectively in multicultural settings. Experience with relocation or working in diverse teams is a plus.
- Include International Experience: If you have any prior experience working overseas, traveling, or engaging with international organizations, include it on your resume to demonstrate your global competency.
- Highlight Relevant Skills: Federal jobs overseas often require skills such as language proficiency, cross-cultural communication, or familiarity with foreign regulations. Make sure to showcase any relevant skills that would make you an asset in an international environment.

19.3 Compensation and Benefits for Federal Employees Overseas

Federal employees stationed overseas enjoy a range of benefits, including competitive pay, housing allowances, and tax advantages. Understanding the full compensation package is key to evaluating job offers and making informed decisions about accepting overseas positions.

19.3.1 Overseas Pay Structures and Allowances

Federal employees working abroad are generally compensated under the General Schedule (GS) or other federal pay scales, with additional allowances for living expenses and other costs related to working overseas.

Key Components of Overseas Compensation:
- Base Pay: Your base salary is determined by the GS grade of your position, which is similar to domestic positions.
- Post Allowance (Cost of Living Allowance): This allowance is designed to cover the higher cost of living in foreign countries. The amount depends on the country, your family size, and local living costs.
- Living Quarters Allowance (LQA): LQA covers the cost of housing for federal employees overseas. It may include rent, utilities, and maintenance costs. Not all positions offer LQA, so confirm with the hiring agency.
- Post Differential: For employees stationed in hardship locations, the government may offer a post differential, which provides additional pay based on the difficulty of living conditions in the assigned country.

19.3.2 Tax Benefits and Exemptions

U.S. federal employees working overseas may be eligible for tax benefits and exemptions, including the Foreign Earned Income Exclusion (FEIE), which allows a portion of your income to be excluded from federal taxes if you meet certain residency requirements.

Tax Benefits to Consider:
- Foreign Earned Income Exclusion (FEIE): You may exclude up to a certain amount of your foreign earnings from federal income tax if you qualify under the residency or physical presence test.
- Tax-Free Allowances: Many of the allowances you receive for housing, living expenses, and cost of living adjustments are tax-exempt, which can significantly reduce your tax burden.

19.4 Preparing for Life and Work Abroad

Working overseas comes with logistical and personal challenges, from understanding the relocation process to adjusting to a new culture and environment. Being well-prepared will help you succeed both personally and professionally in your new role.

19.4.1 Navigating the Relocation Process

Relocating for a federal job overseas involves more than just packing up and moving—it requires understanding your agency's relocation assistance policies, coordinating logistics, and ensuring that your personal affairs are in order before departure.

Steps to Prepare for Relocation:
- Review Relocation Benefits: Some agencies offer relocation allowances that cover the cost of moving household goods, travel expenses, and temporary lodging. Be sure to confirm what's covered in your offer.
- Plan for Family and Dependents: If you're relocating with your family, make sure to consider schooling for children, healthcare options, and employment opportunities for your spouse if applicable.
- Health and Immunizations: Depending on the country you're moving to, you may need vaccinations or health screenings. Check the CDC guidelines for your destination.

19.4.2 Adapting to a New Culture

Living and working abroad requires flexibility and openness to different customs, languages, and cultural practices. Adapting to your new environment will make the transition smoother and improve your experience as an overseas employee.

Tips for Cultural Adaptation:
- Learn the Language: Even if you're not fluent, learning basic phrases in the local language can help you communicate better and show respect for the local culture. Many federal installations offer language classes, or you can use apps like Duolingo or Babbel to build basic language skills.
- Respect Local Customs: Take the time to learn about the cultural norms, traditions, and etiquette in your host country. Being aware of local customs can help you avoid misunderstandings and demonstrate cultural sensitivity.
- Connect with the Local Community: Engage with both the local and expatriate communities. Building relationships with locals can enrich your experience, while connecting with other expats can provide a support network as you adjust to life abroad.

19.4.3 Managing Personal Well-Being Abroad

Living overseas can be exciting, but it also comes with challenges like homesickness, isolation, and adjusting to a new environment. Taking care of your mental and physical health is essential to thriving in your new role.

Maintaining Well-Being While Overseas:
- Stay Connected to Home: Use technology to maintain regular communication with family and friends back home. Video calls, messaging apps, and social media can help reduce feelings of isolation.
- Establish a Routine: Developing a daily routine can create a sense of normalcy in a foreign environment. Whether it's exercise, work, or hobbies, having a routine can help you feel more settled.
- Access to Healthcare: Be sure to understand how healthcare services work in your host country, including accessing medical care on base or through local providers.

Federal employees often have access to high-quality healthcare through the Federal Employees Health Benefits (FEHB) program.

19.5 Leveraging Available Resources for Overseas Employees

Federal employees working overseas have access to various resources and support networks to assist with their professional and personal transitions. These resources can help you navigate the challenges of living abroad and connect with the broader federal community.

19.5.1 Support from U.S. Embassies and Consulates

If you're stationed in a country with a U.S. embassy or consulate, these offices can provide support for U.S. citizens, including federal employees. They often host social events, provide emergency services, and offer a range of resources for expatriates.

How Embassies and Consulates Can Assist:
- Emergency Services: In the event of a natural disaster, political unrest, or medical emergency, U.S. embassies and consulates offer support and guidance for U.S. citizens living abroad.
- Social and Networking Events: Many embassies and consulates host social events, including Fourth of July celebrations, professional networking opportunities, and cultural exchange programs.
- Community Resources: Embassies and consulates often provide information about local healthcare, legal services, and education resources for families.

19.5.2 Military Base Support for Civilian Employees

If you're working on or near a U.S. military base overseas, you may have access to many of the same support services as military personnel and their families. These services can provide valuable resources for adjusting to life abroad and finding a sense of community.

Base Services for Civilians:
- Commissaries and Exchanges: Civilians working on military installations often have access to on-base commissaries and exchanges, which provide goods and services similar to what you would find in the U.S.
- Healthcare Services: Many bases offer medical and dental services for civilian employees and their families. Be sure to verify your eligibility for on-base healthcare through your employing agency.
- Recreation and Leisure Activities: Most U.S. military bases provide recreational facilities such as gyms, pools, and organized sports. Participating in these activities can help you stay active and meet other expats.

19.6 Returning to the U.S. After an Overseas Assignment

After working overseas, many federal employees will eventually return to the U.S., either by choice or through the natural end of their assignment. It's important to plan ahead for your transition back to the U.S. to ensure a smooth reintegration into the domestic workforce and daily life.

19.6.1 Navigating Reassignment or Repatriation

When your overseas assignment ends, you may have the option to transfer to a new position within the U.S. or return to a previous role. Planning your reassignment or repatriation ahead of time will help you make a seamless transition.

Steps for Returning to the U.S.:
1. Work with HR on Reassignment: Contact your agency's human resources department to discuss available positions in the U.S. if you're looking for a new role. Federal agencies often offer assistance with reassignment or repatriation for employees returning from overseas.
2. Plan for Relocation Logistics: Moving back to the U.S. after an overseas assignment can be as complex as your initial relocation. Be sure to coordinate with your agency on shipping household goods, travel arrangements, and temporary housing if needed.
3. Consider Reverse Culture Shock: Returning to the U.S. after living abroad can be an adjustment, particularly if you've spent several years overseas. Prepare for some initial discomfort as you readjust to life in the U.S.

19.6.2 Leveraging Overseas Experience for Career Advancement

Your overseas experience is a valuable asset that can help advance your federal career, especially if you're looking for leadership positions or roles that require international expertise.

How to Leverage Your Overseas Experience:
- Highlight International Skills: Emphasize the cross-cultural communication, adaptability, and leadership skills you developed while working overseas on your resume and during interviews.
- Pursue Roles with International Focus: Consider applying for federal positions that involve international relations, foreign policy, or defense, where your overseas experience will be particularly relevant.
- Network with Colleagues from Your Overseas Assignment: Stay in touch with the professional contacts you made during your time abroad. These connections can lead to future job opportunities or mentorship in international roles.

Conclusion

Applying for federal employment overseas offers a unique opportunity for career advancement, personal growth, and the chance to experience life in different parts of the world. Whether you're a civilian, a veteran, a military spouse, or a service member transitioning to civilian life, federal jobs abroad provide stability, competitive benefits, and valuable international experience.

By understanding the overseas hiring process, preparing for the challenges of living and working abroad, and leveraging available resources, you can successfully navigate this exciting career opportunity. Be sure to research the pay structures, benefits, and job requirements specific to federal positions overseas, and approach your relocation with a well-thought-out plan to ensure a smooth transition.

Chapter 20: Understanding the Priority Placement Program (PPP) for Federal Employment

The federal government offers several programs to assist federal employees and military spouses in securing employment. One of the most significant and beneficial of these programs is the Priority Placement Program (PPP). The PPP is designed to help displaced federal employees, military spouses, and other eligible individuals find employment within the federal system, particularly after relocation or other employment disruptions. The program helps ensure that eligible employees have priority consideration for open positions, providing a crucial safety net during times of transition.

In this chapter, we will explore the ins and outs of the Priority Placement Program, how it works, who is eligible, and the steps you need to take to use it effectively in your federal employment journey.

20.1 What is the Priority Placement Program (PPP)?

The Priority Placement Program (PPP) is a Department of Defense (DoD) program that gives eligible individuals priority consideration for federal positions, primarily focusing on helping displaced employees and military spouses. The program helps to minimize the disruption caused by relocation, base closures, downsizing, or other employment challenges by placing affected employees in new roles across federal agencies. While it primarily benefits DoD employees, certain aspects of the program apply to other federal agencies as well.

20.1.1 Purpose of the PPP

The PPP aims to assist several groups, including:
- Displaced Federal Employees: Those who have lost or are about to lose their jobs due to reductions in force (RIF), base closures, or realignment.
- Military Spouses: Spouses of military service members who are relocating due to Permanent Change of Station (PCS) orders, or who are affected by the disability or death of a service member.
- Wounded Warriors and Veterans: Certain veterans and wounded service members may also benefit from priority placement.

The program allows these individuals to receive preference over other candidates when applying for certain federal positions, helping to provide job security and ensure that experienced federal workers are retained in the system.

20.2 Eligibility for the Priority Placement Program

Understanding your eligibility for the PPP is critical to taking full advantage of the program. Several categories of individuals may be eligible, including federal employees facing displacement, military spouses, and certain veterans.

20.2.1 Categories of Eligible Employees

Several categories of individuals qualify for the Priority Placement Program. These include:
- Displaced DoD Employees: Federal employees who are facing job loss due to a reduction in force (RIF), closure of their duty station, or realignment of duties within the DoD are eligible for priority placement. Employees may also be eligible if their position is eliminated due to base closures or realignments.
- Military Spouses: Spouses of active-duty service members who are relocating due to a Permanent Change of Station (PCS) or who have been affected by the disability or death of a service member may qualify for priority placement. Spouses who are relocating to follow their military spouse to a new duty station are often in need of employment in the new location, and the PPP provides a critical pathway to securing federal work.

20.2.2 Criteria for Military Spouse Preference

Military spouses can face significant disruptions to their careers due to frequent relocations. The PPP provides military spouses with hiring preferences when their family relocates due to a PCS move or when they are otherwise displaced.

To be eligible, military spouses must:
- Have moved to a new duty station due to a PCS order.
- Be married to an active-duty service member.
- Be applying for a position within a reasonable commuting distance from the service member's new duty station.

Military spouses should apply within the relevant timeframes after a PCS move, as eligibility is time-sensitive. The priority preference does not guarantee placement, but it significantly increases the likelihood of being hired.

20.2.3 Eligibility for Veterans and Wounded Warriors

Veterans who are disabled or have been affected by base realignments may also be eligible for the PPP. Specific categories of veterans and wounded service members may qualify for priority consideration based on their service-connected disabilities or special hiring authorities.

20.3 How the Priority Placement Program Works

The Priority Placement Program is a well-structured system that matches eligible individuals with available federal job openings. The program helps eligible individuals access job opportunities across the federal government, giving them a leg up over other applicants by prioritizing their placement.

20.3.1 Registration in the Program

To take advantage of the PPP, eligible individuals must first register in the system. The registration process varies depending on your eligibility category, but it typically involves providing documentation that proves eligibility (such as PCS orders or RIF notices).

Steps to Register:
1. Gather Documentation: For displaced employees, this may include your RIF notice or other documentation proving that your position is being eliminated. For military spouses, PCS orders and proof of marriage are typically required.
2. Contact Human Resources: If you are a federal employee, your HR office will help you register in the PPP system. For military spouses, your installation's Family Support Center or the Civilian Personnel Office can assist with the process.
3. Complete the Application: Once your eligibility is confirmed, you will complete the PPP registration, which may include selecting the types of positions and locations you are willing to work in.

20.3.2 Job Matching and Placement Process

Once you are registered in the PPP, the system will automatically match you with available positions based on your qualifications, location preferences, and other factors. When a suitable position becomes available, you will be referred to the hiring manager for priority consideration.

Key Features of the Matching Process:
- Automatic Matching: The PPP system searches for open positions that match your skills, experience, and location preferences. Eligible candidates are automatically matched with positions that fit their profile.
- Priority Consideration: Once you are matched with a job opening, your application is prioritized over other applicants. This gives you a significant advantage in securing the position.
- Job Offer: If the hiring manager determines that you are a good fit for the role, you will receive a job offer. You may be required to undergo an interview or complete additional assessments, but your priority status puts you ahead of other candidates in the process.

20.3.3 Military Spouse Employment Preferences (PPP-S)

Military spouses enrolled in the Priority Placement Program (PPP-S) have access to a streamlined process for finding federal jobs after a PCS move. The PPP-S program provides them with priority referral for positions within the commuting area of the new duty station.

How Military Spouse PPP-S Works:
- Eligibility for PPP-S: Military spouses become eligible when they relocate due to PCS orders and can register for the PPP-S system through the Civilian Personnel Office or Family Support Center at their new installation.
- Job Referrals: Once registered, military spouses are referred for open federal positions that match their qualifications within the new location.
- Renewal of Eligibility: Military spouses can continue to be eligible for PPP-S as long as they meet the conditions set out in the PCS orders and the specific timeframes for preference applications.

20.4 Benefits of the Priority Placement Program

The PPP provides several benefits to federal employees, military spouses, and other eligible individuals. These benefits go beyond simply providing priority in the hiring process; the program also offers security and career continuity during times of transition.

20.4.1 Job Security During Transition

For federal employees facing job loss due to reductions in force or base closures, the PPP offers critical job security. By placing displaced workers into new roles, the program helps avoid prolonged periods of unemployment and allows workers to continue their federal careers with minimal disruption.

20.4.2 Support for Military Spouses

The PPP-S component of the program offers military spouses a critical resource as they relocate frequently with their active-duty partners. With priority placement, military spouses can more easily secure federal employment, reducing career disruptions and providing stability for their families.

20.4.3 Career Continuity

The PPP helps eligible individuals maintain their careers without significant gaps in employment. For federal workers displaced by downsizing, or military spouses moving to a new location, the program ensures that they have a pathway to continue their professional growth.

20.5 Tips for Maximizing the Benefits of PPP

To make the most of the Priority Placement Program, it's essential to understand how to navigate the system and take full advantage of the available resources.

20.5.1 Be Proactive in Registration

Don't wait until the last minute to register for the PPP. As soon as you know you will be eligible, begin gathering the necessary documentation and work with your HR office or installation support center to register as quickly as possible. Early registration increases your chances of finding a suitable placement.

20.5.2 Be Flexible with Location and Roles

The more flexible you are in terms of the locations and roles you are willing to accept, the more opportunities you will have in the program. Consider broadening your job preferences to increase your chances of finding a placement.

20.5.3 Stay Engaged with HR and Support Services

Keep in close contact with your HR office or Family Support Center to ensure you remain informed about new opportunities. They can also help guide you through the registration and placement process, making it easier for you to navigate the system.

Conclusion

The Priority Placement Program (PPP) offers a vital safety net for displaced federal employees, military spouses, and other eligible individuals, helping them secure new federal employment during times of transition. Whether you're a federal employee facing a reduction in force or a military spouse relocating due to a PCS order, the PPP provides an invaluable tool for ensuring career continuity and financial stability.

By understanding how the PPP works, who is eligible, and the steps needed to register, you can take full advantage of the program to secure your next federal job. Whether you're navigating a career transition or seeking employment at a new duty station, the Priority Placement Program helps smooth the process, allowing you to focus on your next steps without the stress of prolonged job searches or employment gaps.

By leveraging the support available through the PPP, displaced federal employees and military spouses can access a broad range of federal jobs that match their skills and preferences. Staying proactive, being flexible, and maintaining engagement with your HR or personnel office will maximize your chances of securing a new position in a timely manner.

Made in the USA
Columbia, SC
04 November 2024